HOMOSEXUALITY
and the
CATHOLIC CHURCH

HOMOSEXUALITY and the CATHOLIC CHURCH

edited by
Jeannine Gramick

THE THOMAS MORE PRESS

Chicago, Illinois

ISBN 0-88347-149-3

ACKNOWLEDGMENTS

The editor and publisher are grateful to the following for permission to print copyrighted material:

Excerpt from "Our Vulnerability Needs Ministry" by Anthony Padovano, October 23, 1981 *National Catholic Reporter.* Reprinted by permission of the *National Catholic Reporter,* P.O. Box 281, Kansas City, MO 64141.

Excerpt from SEXUAL STIGMA: *An Interactionist Account* by K. Plummer. Copyright 1975. Reprinted by permission of Routledge & Kegan Paul, Ltd., Boston, MA.

Excerpt from HOMOSEXUALITY AND THE CHRISTIAN WAY OF LIFE by Edward Malloy. Reprinted by permission of University Press of America.

Excerpt from "Ongoing Growth Through Intimacy" by Peter Cantwell, Vol. 2, No. 3, Fall, 1981 issue of *Human Development.* Reprinted by permission of Human Development, New York, NY.

Excerpt from "Catholic Homosexuals" by Gregory Baum, Vol. 99, No. 19 issue of *Commonweal.* Reprinted by permission of Commonweal, New York, NY.

Dedicated to Robert Nugent, friend and colleague, a rare human being who makes me laugh and helps me to realize that life and work should be taken seriously, but not too seriously.

Contents

(*Continued*)

Contents

Preface

SEXUALITY and religion have always been intimately and powerfully linked throughout human history. How we perceive and experience the one profoundly affects our feelings about the other. Religious systems which interpret reality have historically conditioned the meanings, values and expressions we assign to human sexual behavior in all known civilizations. Specific sexual activities have either been encouraged and supported in accord with the belief system or have been discouraged and condemned as opposed to it.

One particular form of human sexual behavior that has always proved of great concern to individuals and to social groupings is homosexuality. In the past ten years homosexuality has been receiving increasingly more and more attention. In popular publications and newspapers, in professional and technical journals of religion, psychiatry, and psychology, in the health professions and allied fields, articles and studies have explored almost all possible forms of the multifaceted phenomenon we call homosexuality. A large portion of this research and interest has focused on the lifestyles of individual lesbian and gay persons, their group culture and subcultures, their personal and social problems.

Until recently churches have continued to view homosexuality in light of ancient taboos, fears and anxieties which the topic so often generates. Ecclesiastical leaders have slipped into the convenience of simply ignoring the subject. However, the last decade has witnessed a significant shift in attitudes from many segments within the U.S. Catholic Church.

In 1969 an organization called Dignity was begun as a spiritual support group for lesbian and gay Catholics. Like the mustard seed that Jesus spoke of in the synoptic gospels, Dignity blossomed in dioceses across the United States and forced church hierarchy to deal with the issue of homosexuality. By 1982 eight dioceses had established some official outreach to the lesbian and gay community. Several Catholic bishops in the United States have issued pastoral statements on the subject, the bishops of England and Wales have produced a set of guidelines for pastoral ministry with homosexual Catholics, and the bishops of the Netherlands are circulating a discussion document, *Homosexual People in Society*.

In 1977 another organization which would move the homosexual issue into a more public forum in the Catholic Church was founded. The group, New Ways Ministry, would provide an educational locus to enable the non-gay community to learn more about the hidden minority within our church and society. In the latter 1970s many peace and justice groups began to acknowledge that civil and human rights are also the birthright of homosexual people. Approximately 3,000 Catholics had publicly endorsed a statement supporting civil rights for lesbian and gay people. In addition, religious congregations of women and men were beginning to deal openly and honestly with the homosexual members in their midst.

In their 1976 pastoral letter on moral values, *To Live in Christ Jesus,* the U.S. Catholic bishops stated that "the Christian community should provide them (homosexual persons) a special degree of pastoral understanding and care." In order to provide for such pastoral ministry, church leaders began to accept the responsibility to become educated to the special problems involved in this sensitive issue. In addition to calling for "education in human sexuality," the U.S. bishops, in their plan of pastoral action for family ministry, "A Vision and a Strategy," encouraged ministers "to acquire specialized skills for dealing with such complex issues as poverty, aging, alcoholism, drug abuse and homosexuality."

Evidence of an attitudinal shift within the Catholic Church in the 1970s from fear and silence to openness and inquiry was the convergence of more than 150 national and diocesan church leaders in Washington, D.C., November 20–22, 1981, for the First National Symposium on Homosexuality and the Catholic Church. The purpose of the symposium was to provide national and diocesan leadership with basic and solid information regarding homosexuality from the perspective of sociology, moral, pastoral and feminist theology, religious life and celibacy, as well as from the experience of lesbian and gay persons themselves. Academic in nature, the symposium facilitated a free exchange of information. There was no strategy for action; no advocacy or political positions were espoused.

Before the symposium weekend arrived, the conference planners had to deal with an unforeseen complication. On October 22, 1981, the symposium site was transferred to the National 4-H Center because Holy Trinity Mission Seminary, the original site, could not accommodate the unexpectedly large number of preregistrants. After planning with the 4-H Center staff, New Ways Ministry received a letter on November 5, 1981 indicating that the conference did not "appear to meet the guidelines for use of the Center." Specific guidelines such as "jobs, careers, and economics; leadership; citizenship development; etc." were cited in the letter of denial of the facilities. The objectives of the symposium had been noted on the application forms. The symposium did, in fact, meet the guidelines with respect to leadership. Furthermore, other religious groups such as the Methodist Church, the National Catholic Conference for Interracial Justice, and the Campaign for Human Development, had used the same facilities for similar meetings of religious leadership.

This action on the part of the National 4-H Center illustrates a powerful and unfortunate truth: Not only do gay and lesbian people themselves suffer discrimination and injustice, but even non-gay people, who would gather as a community of concerned Christians, also feel the sting of arbitrary and fear-filled decisions designed to prevent them from academically discussing a contemporary social problem. This act of rejection helped the participants to identify with the injustice that homosexual people experience in our society and in our church.

We cannot afford to acquiesce to live in a society and church which can arbitrarily prevent free, adult people from gathering to discuss issues that affect their lives and the lives of millions of others. If we do, then we contribute to the oppression which the gospel calls us to oppose no matter where we find it.

Therefore, New Ways Ministry, the sponsoring organization, pursued legal action to counter the blatant act of discrimination. On November 10, 1981, Ronald Bogard, Esq., legal counsel for New Ways Ministry, filed suit in U.S. District Court. The suit claimed that the National 4-H Center and the U.S. Department of Agriculture, to which the National 4-H Center is closely linked, violated New Ways Ministry's First and Fifth Amendment rights of freedom of speech, assembly, association and equal protection under the law.

The First and Fifth Amendments do not apply to acts of private persons or entities. In order for constitutional provisions to be involved, the court had to find that there was a sufficiently strong connection between the National 4-H Center and the federal government; in this case, the U.S. Department of Agriculture. On August 31, 1982, U.S. District Judge Barrington Parker ruled that a sufficient connection did not exist.

Unfortunately, Judge Barrington Parker's ruling illustrates how the letter of the law can be observed while its spirit is not. In preliminary hearings the attorneys for both the National 4-H Center and the U.S. Department of Agriculture concurred with Judge Parker that New Ways Ministry had been the recipient of discriminatory action. In most states, however, there is as yet no protective legislation which would preclude discriminatory actions based on the issue of homosexuality. This case represents another example of the need for civil rights legislation concerning homosexual persons and homosexual issues.

Despite the refusal of the National 4-H Center to host the symposium on its grounds, the First National Symposium on Homosexuality and the Catholic Church did take place. It was held at a downtown hotel in Washington, D.C. More than three quarters of the conference registrants were brothers, sisters, or priests from 50 different religious congregations and dioceses. About half of the participants were major superiors of their religious communities or were involved in community vocation or formation work. The remaining participants were educational administrators, psychologists, counselors, doctors, attorneys, parish ministers, campus ministers or representatives of national or diocesan Catholic organizations. About 8% of the participants were members of Dignity. The participants came from 31 different states and Canada and were equally divided between women and men. Such a profile of the conference participants indicates that a broad representation of Catholic religious leadership gave serious consideration and study to the sensitive subject of homosexuality and its impact on the Catholic Church in contemporary society. Faith, prayer, and worship provided the context in which the listening, questioning and dialogue during the symposium took place.

The chapters contained in this book are based on presentations given at this First National Symposium on Homosexuality and the Catholic Church. All well qualified in their respective fields, the conference speakers contributed further insights and developments in the area of sexuality which can benefit many more individuals than those who attended the symposium. It is with this purpose of fostering greater dialogue on the subject of homosexuality in the Catholic Church that these papers are made available to the general public.

Varying in style and content, some of the eight chapters are highly academic or technical while others are based on personal experience. The book is divided into two sections: sociological perspectives and ecclesial perspectives. The ordering of the two sections is extremely significant. Before a proper evaluation of the homosexual person or homosexual behavior can be rendered in a religious or theological context, it is imperative to understand the social fabric from which the lesbian or gay person emerges. Such a principle holds true in examining any moral problem. It is important that any study of homosexuality is begun by listening to the personal stories of lesbian and gay persons and by informing ourselves with available knowledge from psychology, anthropology, biology, and other social science disciplines.

The first two chapters are personal accounts of how it feels to grow up lesbian or gay and also Catholic. One from a man's and the other from a woman's point of view, the companion pieces help the reader to feel some of the pain and loneliness associated with being young and feeling physically attracted to one's own gender. In a light, humorous and anecdotal vein, Brian McNaught and Ann Borden also communicate why they like being who they are. As one gay activist poster puts it, "God made us and God doesn't make junk!".

The chapters on new sociological theory, feminism and morality are written in a more philosophical or theoretical style. Building upon personal experience, these papers systematically propose a framework from which logical deductions are made, inconsistencies, errors or injustices are noted, and crucial questions are posed. My sociological analysis invites further theological development and reexamination in the light of contemporary knowledge. Barbara Zanotti's chapter on feminism points out the underlying connection between the women's movement and the gay liberation movement: the heterosexual norm of male control over women. Charles Curran critiques four moral positions and presents his own based on his methodology of compromise.

The remaining three chapters address the issue of homosexuality as it relates to religious life and the priesthood. "Civil Rights in a Church of Compassion" by Theresa Kane and Cornelius Hubbuch's article, "Gay Men and the Vowed Life," represent two different responses to Robert Nugent's lengthy treatment of celibacy and homosexuality. Each response appropriately comes from a former official of the Leadership Conference of Women Religious and the Conference of Major Superiors of Men.

The authors in this volume speak to us as theologians, ministers and educators, but most of all they speak to us as our sisters and brothers in the church. They are not proposing simple solutions but are helping us to ask some penetrating questions. They are not condemning nor confronting but are engaging us in a healthy dialogue. For this reason alone they deserve a hearing and a response from all of us who are deeply concerned about our lesbian sisters and our gay brothers.

It is my deepest hope that their genuine concern in this area will be met with an equally genuine response from all of us who hear them. They have helped us take the first step toward that "calm, careful study, prayer and reflection" about which Archbishop Rembert Weakland of Milwaukee speaks in his July, 1980 pastoral, "Who Is Our Neighbor?". He reminds us that all people have basic God-given rights and that they should not be treated as outcasts, as second-class citizens or as somehow contaminated. Like Jesus, Archbishop Weakland invites us to "come write in the sand with me. Who is going to throw the first stone?".

Jeannine Gramick, SSND
Mt. Rainier, Maryland
September 23, 1982

Acknowledgments

SPONSORED by New Ways Ministry, the First National Symposium on Homosexuality and the Catholic Church would not have occurred without the financial, moral and physical support of numerous individuals and groups. Although the local ordinary, Archbishop James A. Hickey, did not approve the conference, 43 national or diocesan Catholic organizations did endorse it. Symposium endorsement was a public statement of the need to provide an open forum for discussion of the issue of homosexuality and the church. Such endorsement did not imply that the speakers' views were necessarily those of the endorsing organizations. The names of the endorsing organizations are listed below.

Undoubtedly much work went into the preparation and execution of the symposium and the present book. Special thanks are in order to Joseph Izzo, CFX, for his excellent facilitation of the symposium, to Ronald Bogard, Esq., for his legal assistance and expertise, to Diann Neu, SP, Ann D'Alessandro, CNZ, Helen Rousseau, CNZ, Art Lavoie, Tom Hlas, Carol Coston, OP, and Michael Guinan, OFM for their leadership in prayer and liturgical celebrations during the symposium. I wish to thank Rick Garcia, Joe Orndorff, Joe Bekisz, Janet O'Connor and Jack O'Connor, long-time supporters of

New Ways Ministry, for their invaluable help during the symposium. I especially wish to thank Tom Hlas, my friend and co-worker, for his many hours of typing, reviewing the manuscripts, and general administration required to bring this book to you. And of course, I shall always thank Bob Nugent, my co-director at New Ways Ministry, for his challenges and steadfast support for more than 10 years in pastoral outreach to the lesbian and gay community. Without such a solid rock to rely on, I would not have been able to coordinate the First National Symposium on Homosexuality and the Catholic Church nor to compile these manuscripts for your reflection.

J. G.

ENDORSERS OF THE FIRST NATIONAL SYMPOSIUM ON HOMOSEXUALITY AND THE CATHOLIC CHURCH

Administrative Council of the Pittsburgh Sisters of Mercy, Pittsburgh, Pennsylvania
Association of Chicago Priests, Chicago, Illinois
Christian Brothers De La Salle Institute, Moraga, California
Claretian Eastern Province, Oak Park, Illinois
Dominican Sisters of Sparkill, Executive Team, Sparkill, New York
Eighth Day Center for Justice, Chicago, Illinois
Franciscan Province of the Sacred Heart, St. Louis, Missouri
Glenmary Commission on Justice, Neon, Kentucky
The Institute for Peace and Justice, St. Louis, Missouri
Institute of Women Today, Chicago, Illinois
Milwaukee Justice and Peace Center, Milwaukee, Wisconsin
Missionary Oblates of Mary Immaculate, Western Province, Oakland, California

National Assembly of Religious Brothers, Hayward, California
National Assembly of Women Religious, Chicago, Illinois
National Coalition of American Nuns, Chicago, Illinois
National Conference of Religious Vocation Directors of Men (NCRVDM), Chicago, Illinois
National Federation of Priests' Councils, Chicago, Illinois
National Sisters Vocation Conference, Chicago, Illinois
P.A.D.R.E.S., Kansas City, Kansas
Parish Evaluation Project, Chicago, Illinois
Paulist Social Action Committee, Storrs, Connecticut
Quixote Center, Mt. Rainier, Maryland
Religious Formation Conference, Washington, D.C.
School Sisters of Notre Dame, Chicago Provincial Council, Berwyn, Illinois
School Sisters of Notre Dame Provincial Council, Northeastern Province, Wilton, Connecticut
School Sisters of Notre Dame Provincial Team, Baltimore Province, Baltimore, Maryland
Sisters of Charity of Nazareth, Nazareth, Kentucky
Sisters of the Holy Family General Council, Mission San Jose, California
Sisters of the Holy Names, Spokane, Washington
Sisters of Mercy, Province of Detroit, Farmington Hills, Michigan
Sisters of Mercy of Rochester, New York, Executive Council
Sisters of Mercy of the Union, General Administrative Team, Silver Spring, Maryland
Sisters of Notre Dame de Namur, Boston Province Team, Boston, Massachusetts
Sisters of Notre Dame de Namur, California Provincial Team, Saratoga, California
Sisters of St. Dominic, Tacoma, Washington
Sisters of St. Joseph of Carondelet, Provincial Council, St. Louis Province
Sisters of St. Joseph, Cleveland, Administrative Staff, Cleveland, Ohio
Sisters of St. Joseph of Peace, Justice and Peace Office, Washington, D.C.
Sisters of St. Joseph of Peace, St. Mary Provincialate, Bellevue, Washington, D.C.

Society of the Divine Savior Provincial Team, American Province
Washington Theological Union, Silver Spring, Maryland
Women's Ordination Conference
Xaverian Brothers, American Central Province, Kensington, Maryland

PART ONE

Sociological Perspectives

Chapter One

REFLECTIONS OF A GAY CATHOLIC

Brian McNaught

I AM the product of an upper middle class, white, Irish Catholic background. I am very happily involved in a long-term relationship. I own an Irish setter named Jeremy and a white canary named Bing Crosby. My partner, Ray, is a money market trader and together we live in Brookline, Massachusetts. I write from that perspective.

I do not speak for black gay people, male or female. I do not speak for Jewish gay people; their experiences are totally different. Many of the things that happened in my life also happened in theirs, but it is essential that one realizes that this chapter, and the one by Ann Borden which follows, represent only our two personal perspectives. They do not tell the story that every gay person needs to tell for himself or herself.

It is important to hear our personal stories if one wishes to understand homosexuality because the oppression associated with homosexuality, unlike any other issue involving a minority group today, is predominantly psychological as opposed to physical. We whites, who were involved in the black civil rights movement or who boycotted grapes and lettuce with Cesar Chavez, did so because we witnessed the economic squalor that blacks and farm workers were facing. We were enraged by sights of police dogs attacking people in Selma, Alabama. We were moved to action by seeing the poverty of the vineyards. It is difficult, however, for gay people, as a whole, to present pictures of economic deprivation as evidence of our oppression.

It is also difficult for gay people to get the support of interested heterosexual men and women without risking the loss of their sexual identity. I could march in a black pride parade and maintain my identity as a privileged white male, but you can not march with gay people and maintain your heterosexual identity unless, of course, you wear a button which says "Straight and Proud!" It is very difficult to get people to join with us because they cannot publicly preserve their heterosexual identity and they do not sufficiently understand the issue.

Some people, for instance, believe that homosexuality is a choice and as such, believe that it can be "unchosen." In other words, one's minority status is perceived as self-chosen. Others presume that homosexuality dawns on an individual post-puberty or after one's sixteenth birthday. On the contrary, homosexuality is something that is generally apparent to the male from the earliest moment that he can remember. There is no choice involved. The horror that I want to share with you is the horror of growing up alone. I will do that from a Catholic perspective because that is an essential part of my story.

In 1948 and 1953, Alfred Kinsey shocked the world with his study of sexuality. Prior to that, it was believed that almost everybody was exclusively heterosexual in their response except for a few homosexual people. On an arbitrary scale from 0 to 6 Kinsey showed that a large segment of the population is exclusively heterosexual (category 0) in their psychosexual response. More importantly, he illustrated that at least ten percent of the population falls into categories 4, 5, or 6, representing those persons who are exclusively homosexual or predominantly homosexual with some heterosexual fantasies or activities.

Kinsey also showed that an enormous segment of the population falls between categories 1 and 5 in this sexual orientation continuum. He revealed that 37 percent of American men have homosexual experiences, post-puberty, to the point of orgasm and that 50 percent of American men have homosexual fantasies. In addition, 20 percent of American women have homosexual experiences. Thus a significant percentage of the population is dealing with homosexual feelings in their own lives. In addition, when a child shares with the family the fact that he or she is a homosexual person, the entire family, including about 44 million parents, is affected.

The modern gay movement did not begin in this country until 1969 and until that time people really felt a strong pressure to marry. Because of this fact, I believe that the majority of homosexual people in this country today are heterosexually married. When we consider the spouses of homosexual individuals, their parents, siblings, aunts and uncles, we come to realize that a considerable number of people are affected by homosexuality. It has been suggested that every homosexual, male or female, intimately relates to at least ten people in his or her life. Those who are involved in counseling in any way know the truth of this assertion.

There is a greater awareness of homosexuality today.

For the past eight years I have been speaking publicly on the subject. When I first began addressing college and university classes I would ask the audience how many of them knew gay people. I would see only a few raised hands. Today at least three quarters of the audience raise their hands to the surprise of the one quarter who do not. I assure them that they will all be able to raise their hands by the end of the talk!

The terminology generally used for male homosexuality is "gay." Gay is an adjective and not a noun, as in speaking of a gay male or a gay person. It is important not to think of gay as a noun. To do so is an attempt to sum up the entire person with those three letters. There is much more to my life than my homosexuality. Although it is an essential part of who I am, I refuse to be identified solely by my sexual orientation.

A large number of women prefer the term "lesbian." The word derives from Lesbos, a Greek isle where the poetess Sappho taught young women. However, some women do not like the term lesbian just as some gay males do not like the term gay. Generally speaking, however, gay and lesbian are the terms that homosexual people prefer.

One more distinction seems in order. The majority of psychiatrists today insist that a person does not choose his or her sexual orientation and that it is probably determined by unknown factors by no later than age five. Such a situation describes a constitutional homosexual person. On the other hand, a transitional homosexual individual is one who engages in homosexual activity because no members of the opposite gender are available; such as in a prison situation, the armed forces, or sometimes even in religious life. When the transitional homosexual person leaves that setting, he or she will revert to a heterosexual orientation. The director of the federal prison program recently insisted in an internal communication that prison rape should no longer be called "homosexual" rape because almost invariably it is heterosexual individuals raping either unwilling homosexual people or weaker heterosexual persons. The gay prisoners I counseled at Jackson State Prison in Michigan wished to be secluded from the rest of the prisoners because they were being victimized by heterosexual individuals whose behavior we would characterize as transitionally homosexual.

In order to get a sense of the isolation I once experienced, I want to take you on a little fantasy trip. I would like you to think of yourself as a heterosexual male whether you are, in fact, or not. Assume that you are the only heterosexual person in the world and that everyone else is gay.

Like your brothers and sister, you were born into a happy home, have lots of friends, and have aspirations for what you want to be when you grow up. You have same-sexed parents. It is believed that same-sexed parents, because they love each other as equals, would probably provide a better home. It is believed that gay love is the perfect love since a man who loves a man is loving an equal, but a man who loves a woman secretly wishes he was a woman. (A parallel situation holds for women.) You are raised in this same-sexed family and you watch television in which every program and every commercial is same-sex oriented. You see, for instance, two men using Zest and running into the ocean together. All the situation comedies show two men or two women living together. After a short period of time, at a relatively early age, you realize that there is something a little different about you. You can identify with nothing on television, but you are afraid to tell anyone. You are a little boy sitting with your brothers as they talk about how handsome the TV star Robert Conrad is. You are afraid to admit that you are really interested in the attractive woman in the show. Such a foolish admission may risk their censuring you as a *breeder*.

In this society, heterosexual people are called *breeders*. It is presumed that heterosexual people are sick, for they have only one thing on their minds: the procreation of children. Love is not an aspect of sex for them; they are disordered and not loved by God. It is further thought that heterosexual men wished to be women and that heterosexual women wish to be men. By definition, heterosexual individuals are not mentally well.

You are terrified that this may be describing you and your feelings as a third grader. You are terrified of telling anyone about your developing crushes on a woman school teacher. Such a disclosure would result in the loss of your friends and your parent's love. So you keep your secret and you pretend. You fulfill others' homosocial expectations of you to avoid isolation. You date another person of the same gender, attend the expected dances and proms. In order to camouflage your real self, you become involved in school activities. To appease society's hatred for heterosexual people, you boast loudly about how you would beat up a heterosexual person if you ever found one.

In school one day you walk into the john. In a bold, black magic marker the words are written on the wall: "Karen is a breeder." Terrified that one day your name will appear in accusation on the wall, your smokescreen gets even thicker. If you have the opportunity to beat up a suspected breeder, you do so because you desperately want to be one of the guys.

The description of breeders as sick people who are disordered is confusing. Perhaps this describes you. You love people of the opposite sex but you believe your feeling is special. You love God and you can't imagine that God would ever give you a feeling that was not special, that was not OK. You grow up thinking that the world is filled with gay people who are OK, breeders who are sick and disgusting, and you. You are all by yourself. No one in the whole world feels like you do and you better not tell anyone.

In college, one day, you roam downtown and enter a porno bookstore, pay your 50¢ to the man at the counter, and walk into that special section. In a stack of papers, you discover a newspaper for heterosexual people. You get so excited you do not know what to do! You roam around for 20 minutes before you have the nerve to pick it up. You do not read it; you just grab it as well as several gay publications and you tell the man at the counter that you are doing a term paper. In some safe place you read excitedly about the possibility that there are other people in town who feel the same way you do.

This publication reveals the location of a breeder bar in town. Situated in the ghetto (the only safe place since no other neighborhood would tolerate it), the breeder bar is run by the Mafia. You are terrified that all the people your parents warned you about are in that bar. You hate the breeders yet you want to be with them because you want to feel at peace, at home, and accepted.

After three weeks of walking around the block, you

wander into the bar and after plying yourself with gin and tonics, you finally introduce yourself to a woman. She seems to be okay, quite attractive, and laughing a little bit. You make light conversation and are excited to have met someone you might really like.

After a long period of time the two of you develop a strong relationship and nervously decide to rent an apartment even though no landlord wants breeders in his building. When you hug each other at night, you prudently draw the shades, for if your neighbors witnessed your display of goodnight affection, your tires might be flat the next morning.

Nervous and fearful of discovery, the two of you begin to take short secret trips. Christmas at home with your parents is foregone with some manufactured excuse. You fill your home with nice little things—secret statements about the love you share in this dumpy little apartment with your shades drawn. But it is your haven, your heaven.

One day, your special, loved partner is in an accident and is rushed to the emergency room of the nearest hospital. When you arrive, you discover she has been moved to the intensive care unit but you cannot see her because unrelated persons of the opposite sex are not allowed in the ICU. You must make a decision. Do you tell the nurse and doctor that you two are devoted lovers and risk the danger that their anti-straight feelings might be taken out on your partner or do you sit outside fearful of what is going on? You decide to sit and wait. Hours later you are told the unbearable news that your lover of 15 years has died. At the funeral home, your partner's parents ask you to sit in an adjoining parlor because even in death they do not want their daughter disgraced by public knowledge that she was straight.

Please take a few minutes to get in touch with the kinds of feelings you experienced through this fantasy trip. Did you feel anger, fear, loneliness, a sense of isolation, depression? Those are the feelings of many people who grow up gay. I have counseled gay men who have shared various parts of this story with me.

For gay people, growing up alone and terrified of revealing oneself for fear of losing love and respect is the essence of the nightmare. The gay movement today is articulating the fact that we cannot live like that anymore. The alcoholism, suicide and drug addiction rates have been astronomical. Gay people are realizing that we must start affirming ourselves. We must not pretend anymore nor try to conform to roles we will never fit. Trying to be straight for a gay person is unnatural since it is a turning away from natural drives.

My own personal story is the story of a young boy, the middle child of seven Irish Catholics raised in Detroit, who wanted more than anything in the world to be a saint. That was an aspiration which I did not share with too many people! I shared it only with my younger brother, Tommy.

Until recently, my father was a director of public relations for General Motors. He met my mother at the Detroit *Times,* a Hearst newspaper. They married and had seven children. One of the children, a son, died tragically before I was born. I seemed to be a gift to the family from God because of his death. I was the "angel," the promised one, in this Irish Catholic clan in Detroit, and my younger brother Tommy was my "Tonto." The Long Ranger and Tonto shared a room for most of their lives.

I was the one in the family who threw himself against the refrigerator door on Good Friday between 12:00 and

3:00 so no one would eat. I was the one who would remind everyone, as we were traveling and after we had ordered sausage, that it was Friday. I used to tie a towel around my neck and pass out Necco wafers during a pretend home mass. My younger sister, Maureen, would pick the neighbor's flowers for the May altar as Tommy and I set it up. (My younger brother probably wanted to be a saint as much as I.)

The product of 16 years of parochial education, I was identified from the first grade as a real comer. The nuns announced, "This is a prince of a boy." I loved it, as I wanted to be God's best friend. There is nothing in the world I wanted more than to be God's best friend. I thought that being a saint meant pleasing everyone and never upsetting people in authority, especially Sister. If Father took an interest in you, you were really on your way to sainthood. I remember the pyramid in the Baltimore Catechism indicating the levels of holiness. The Pope was at the top followed by priests and religious, selfish married people and then the singles. A saint, however, could leap over the top!

There were little boy saints like Tarsisius who died because he would not allow the other boys to take the holy communion from under his tunic. Tarsisius gave us two messages: are you willing to give up your life for God? and stay away from Protestant boys—they're bullies! Sister told us you could die before puberty and go to heaven like little Johnny who used to go into church every day and say, "Hi, Jesus, this is Johnny." One day Johnny was hit by a car and he heard a voice say, "Hi, Johnny, this is Jesus." You never asked Sister how she had heard that. You knew to accept it in faith.

I believed in Johnny, Tarsisius, in Maria Goretti and,

most of all, in the Chinese martyrs. One day in fifth grade Sister told us about the Chinese who, rather than give up God, had sharpened chopsticks plunged into their ear drums and had their fingernails pulled off. I ran home and after lights were out, I woke up my brother Tommy because Sister said the Red Chinese could be coming up our stairs at any time. He needed to know about these things. We spent two hours discussing a list of tortures we felt we could not endure. The essence of sainthood seemed to be one's willingness to die for God. And for me, growing up meant wanting to be God's best friend, a saint.

At the same time, I was experiencing an inexplicable attraction to men from the earliest moment I can remember. Sitting with my brothers and sisters watching television I would be filled with an intense attraction and preoccupation with the male stars. I had crushes on all of them. I wanted to sleep with Tarzan. I wanted to be held by the life guard and the camp counselors. I felt very, very guilty about these crushes. I had always thought I was a good boy. When it was time to examine my conscience, I did all the things I was taught. Yet, I did not understand *these* feelings and I was afraid to ask anyone about them. I used to look in the World Book Encyclopedia, searching for answers. I found instead pictures of Greek statues. They became my friends.

All my companions at the time were talking about Annette Funicello, the leading mouseketeer on the Mickey Mouse Club. Today she is pushing Skippy peanut butter, but then Annette Funicello was the sexual barometer of my fifth grade. Everyone seemed to love Annette but me. I didn't have the least interest in the bumps under Annette Funicello's sweater. I loved Spin and Marty but I couldn't tell anyone. So, this "best little boy in the world" was very lonely and very isolated. Although I was the kind of boy that my friends' mothers liked to see show up and although I received lots of strokes, inside I was in turmoil.

In high school I was senior class president, and an editor of the yearbook. I had a trophy case of swimming awards and I played basketball. Upon graduation I received the John G. Stewart Christian Leadership Award because I was what the faculty thought every student should be like. After I came out publicly as a gay person eight years later, I heard my name had been removed from the plaque by some faculty member or student. It was replaced, removed again and is now back up only because of one persistent teacher.

Through high school I dated a girl named Carol who had a great sense of humor. She attended the all girls Catholic high school next door to the all boys Catholic high school in which I was enrolled. I felt that perhaps one day I would marry her or the Breck girl and have two children and an English sheep dog like all my friends.

But I was suffering. Not understanding homosexuality, I believed that I was probably the only person in the world who experienced these attractions toward males. I started to hear about faggots, fairies, sissies, fruits, and queers. The high school kids told jokes about Percy and Clarence, two very effeminate men who stood on a bridge and talked to each other about "ferry" boats. I knew they were supposed to be fairies, faggots, queers, sissies. But I did not know that they were also supposed to be homosexual. I thought that fairies, faggots, fruits and sissies were boys who did not want to be boys and who were afraid of sports. I liked being a boy and was not afraid of sports. The only effeminate thing I wore was the surplice and cassock that every altar boy donned for liturgical services. I dreamed about meeting Percy and Clarence on the bridge one night and asking them, "Am I queer?" I didn't understand what was going on with me. I knew that I loved God and my parents and that I wanted to be a saint. But I didn't understand these sexual feelings.

One day in high school the senior class guidance counselor, a religious brother, walked into our honors religion class and said, "If any of you guys come in and tell me you have screwed a chick, I'll talk to you; tell me you are queer and I'll kick you out of the office." That was his pure and simple, unsolicited message. We had not even been discussing homosexuality. So I knew I could not tell even him. I could not tell my parents, my friends, not even Tommy. (It is the one secret I never shared with him.)

Off I went to Marquette University to obtain a journalism degree. I had considered entering religious life for a long time and had announced it three or four times during high school. (I never made decisions without announcing them to everyone!) After my sophomore year I decided to join the Christian Brothers of Ireland and become a teacher. My asking for a guitar for Christmas was evidence that I was serious since those were the days of the singing nun. It was also a sign of true faith to have a guitar, especially if one was going to China! (I have yet to learn how to play it.)

Screening by a psychiatrist was a prerequisite for entrance into the religious community, as the order did not want any strange people! Most of my friends lied but I did not; I told the truth. When the psychiatrist asked, "Is there anything that will make things difficult for you?" I answered, "Yes, I think that I am bisexual." Like stepping into lukewarm water, admitting bisexuality is the first step in "coming out" for many gay people. You still leave a little hope. The person can respond to you with half a smile because there is still half of you that is redeemable. The psychiatrist responded, "Brian, you have had the sexual experience of a twelve year old. I would not worry about it. I think that you will do fine."

Off I went to the monastery and I lasted as long as Maria in "The Sound of Music." After about six weeks, the community and I mutually agreed that discipline was a real issue. (My gerbil got loose in blatant defiance of a house rule barring pets.) The other issue that motivated me to leave the monastery was that I fell in love and it scared me. I was beginning to develop a slight understanding that I was a homosexual. I had never had any heterosexual fantasies and now I was beginning to fall in love with a man and that frightened me. My attitude toward the experience was negative. I felt like I was a pollutant. In olden times, when a homosexual person was buried, he or she was frequently dug up and the bones scattered because it was thought that the body would pollute the area. I was similarly afraid that my love for another man would pollute him.

So I left the monastery and went back to Marquette. As a junior I had a homosexual experience with a freshman in the dorm. The following semester I had to find out if I was really homosexual. I bought a massage book and a six pack of beer and had a sexual experience with an accomplished woman from the state university who lived next door. I knew from that experience, from my fantasy life and from my reactions to men on the street that I must be a homosexual. I did not know any gay people and had never been to a gay bar. I had never read a gay newspaper because I was terrified that, if I walked into a porn shop to buy one, the man behind the counter would instantly turn into Sr. Digna. I quit dating as a senior, admitting that, whatever a homosexual is, that is what I was.

I filed as a conscientious objector in 1970 and was hired by *The Michigan Catholic,* the diocesan newspaper in Detroit, to be a staff writer and weekly columnist. My column became very popular with mothers who would clip it out and scotch tape it to the refrigerator door or mail it to their sons and daughters at college. A frequent mass-goer and lector, I taught students about Jesus after school at one of the local schools. I spoke about Jesus to mother/son or father/daughter communion breakfasts and senior citizens groups. I was known among many people as a young Christian with a mature approach to how religion should be lived and how faith should involve us in civil rights and the major issues of the day. I was involved in every issue except my own and, as such, I felt that I was living a lie.

Two books were incredibly significant for me at that time. One was Hermann Hesse's *Siddhartha* which describes a young man who searches for the meaning of life. On his journey, he encounters the Buddha, the embodiment of truth. Siddhartha's best friend leaves to follow the Buddha but Siddhartha cannot do the same.

My Buddha had been the Church, which I had never questioned except on this sexual issue. This realization began to break the stranglehold that seemed to be around my neck—the struggling with the question of "Am I OK or am I not OK?"

At the same time I was writing the column, I had made my first journey into a gay bar. I met and later developed a relationship with a priest. Together we bought a house in the country. Yet, I could not deal with the inconsistency between my public image and my private life. I was sure that if anyone found out Brian McNaught, the John Boy Walton of Detroit, was living with a priest in a homosexual relationship, I would lose the column and the television show I was hosting on occasion. I would lose the invitations to speak to groups. I would no longer be everyone's favorite Catholic.

The other book of great significance for me was *Francis: The Journey and the Dream,* by Murray Bodo (1972), a Franciscan spiritualist. Francis' journey was the journey into self through which he stripped away all the layers of self-concern: Who am I? How much money do my parents make? How good do I look? Who will remember me when I die? Those were the layers I had accumulated on myself. They were separating me from the divinity within me. Jesus told us that the kingdom of God was within. Francis dreamed that he would come in union with God once he stripped away all the unnecessary levels. He felt that if he could help other people strip away their exterior layers, then all of us would be one in God.

This was my guiding light; this I believed to be true. But I was not living what I believed, I felt I was living a lie. If the essence of the New Testament is to love yourself before you can love anyone else, then loving myself meant that I needed to affirm myself as a gay person and share that affirmation with people. But I was afraid and I was ashamed of the inconsistency between what I felt I was supposed to be doing and what I was actually doing.

Nor was my relationship working out. The priest was 15 years older than I. For each of us, it was our first relationship. As a good Catholic I believed that, if the relationship broke up, I could never have another because I would be divorced. I was afraid that, if I told my parents that the relationship was not working, they would say, "Now will you see a psychiatrist?" So, one lonely Saturday morning when he was out of the house, I drank a bottle of paint thinner. That was going to be my journey home.

I knew that the church considered suicide a mortal sin, but I did not believe that I would go straight to hell because I had always had a very personal relationship with God. God was parent; I was going home to explain to God that I could not hack it. I could not live by the rules. "I do not know what you wanted from me but I could not survive."

So I drank the paint thinner, took some pills, and sat by myself for about a half an hour. In that time I changed my mind, drove myself down the street to the Catholic hospital, and with great difficulty told the nun at the desk that I had tried to commit suicide. The nurses took me into the emergency room and pumped my stomach. With tubes down my nose and throat and with tears running down my cheeks, I swore that I would never again live my life based on other people's expectations of me.

Shortly thereafter I ended the relationship with the priest and began a chapter of Dignity, the gay Catholic group, in Detroit. An inner city apartment was the only meeting space we could afford. Although the meetings were not advertised very well, one by one, people began to walk nervously up a flight of stairs, admitting in that walk, perhaps for the first time, that they were gay. One person told how he had deliberately gained more than one hundred pounds so that he would never have to deal with his sexuality. Another man confessed privately he had stuck his hand in an open flame to punish himself for being homosexual. Another had such an awful twitch when he spoke that it was difficult to understand him. These were gay Catholics I was seeing. But the healing I saw within the small liturgies as we sat on the floor in that inner city apartment convinced me that what I was doing was right and that people needed to know about Dignity.

I took each of the newspaper staff people out to lunch, one by one according to seniority, told them that I was gay, that I wanted to keep that separate from my work, but that I would be working with gay Catholics in Detroit. Each one said that that was no problem. Two weeks later I received a call from the religion editor of the *Detroit News* who wanted to do a feature on homosexuality and religion. At that moment I made what Kierkegaard called a "leap of faith." I knew it would be tremendously embarrassing to my family and that all the signs of my potential sainthood would be lost, but there was no way that the church or other gay people would know what was happening in that apartment room if I ducked the issue. So I consented to the interview. The day after it appeared, my column was dropped.

Several days later a large group of gay people from Ann Arbor picketed outside the *Michigan Catholic*. One of the staff people asked, "Which one of those fairies owes me a quarter for my tooth?"

I understand that it was a difficult time for the newspaper staff. Only in the last several years have I been able to reconcile the pain I felt. These people, my best friends, were not talking to me. Printers were threatening me. Anti-gay articles were posted on the walls of the newspaper building. I realize now that they were frightened; they did not understand. It was 1974.

After two weeks, I decided that there was only one effective way to confront the church I loved with what it was doing to the people I loved and that was to engage in a hunger strike. It was a water fast in reparation of the sins of the church against gay people and I vowed that I would eat no food and drink only water until I received a commitment from the church in Detroit that they would work to educate the clergy. I didn't ask for my column back; I didn't ask for a new official position on homosexuality. I merely wanted the bishops to pledge to educate themselves and the clergy because I knew that gay people had nothing to fear from the truth. As with every other minority struggling for civil rights and respect, our enemy was (is) society's ignorance.

After 24 days, I finally received a letter from the bishops which said they respected the fast and felt they "had a serious obligation to root out those structures and attitudes which discriminate against homosexuals as persons." They also said they would work to educate the clergy and with that promise, I ended my fast. The following day, I was fired from my other responsibilities at the paper.

Since then, I have been working full time with gay people and their families, working to eliminate self-hate and to build self-esteem. I have done so through a syndicated column in the gay press, various writings in the religious press, through lectures and through one-on-one counseling.

One of the critical issues for gay people, I have found, is religion. Even those who maintain they hate religion are basically still struggling with guilt. An enormous number of gay people identify themselves as former Catholics. Gay people who claim a religion and insist that they are still church members are hit from both sides. They are hit by the institutional church which tells them in a variety of ways that they are not welcome. They are likewise hit by a very large and vocal political gay community which tells them that their faith is not welcome.

Gay people who maintain religious ties and who work very hard at becoming part of the institution have only themselves right now. It is a tough road for them. When I am counseling such people, I have them do some homework. I ask them to read current literature because gay people are as ignorant about their own homosexuality as straight people are. We all grew up with the same myths about homosexuality. After reading about the latest findings of social scientists and theologians, I encourage them to join a supportive community.

Before closing, I want to underscore my point about the isolation felt by gay people by sharing with you two letters.

I tackled my first purse snatcher about two months ago. It was exhilarating because the "Percy, Clarence, faggot, sissy, fairy, homosexual" ball of confusion made me feel that perhaps I was not fully male. It has been a real struggle to affirm my masculinity when society has been telling me that I am not a "real" man. I wrote a column about tackling this purse snatcher and how great it made me feel. Then I received the following anonymous letter from a young man in the Washington, D.C. area:

> Your last article particularly hit home to me. I am glad to know that other people were afraid, too. You said that you didn't consider yourself a sissy. I didn't have the choice. It was drummed into me every day of every school year for twelve years. I was a loving, caring person inside but no one looked beyond the way I carried my books and the way I talked. They broke me long before high school graduation and helped to mold me into a very shy and utterly alone human being who needs three drinks now just to get up enough nerve to say 'Hi' to someone in the bars. I am so afraid of people, just terrified. I am in a bad crisis right now. I know people care but the stems of the roses have so many thorns and my fingers are already so sore. Your writing touched me.

He signed it, "A Friend" with a question mark.

Another poignant letter I received talks about the struggle of married homosexual men in the church. One man wrote:

> I have been dealing with this myself all my life, of course, but especially in the last three years. I finally came out to myself a couple of years ago and to a few trusted friends since then. I am 39, married, father of five, an employee in the church in a high level department. I have a long way to go in dealing with this truth with my wife, my children, my parents, brothers and sisters, my employer. I don't have the slightest idea how it is all going to turn out but I trust the same loving God who has brought me this far will help me the rest of the way. . . .

In conclusion, I would like to share with you a selection from my book, *A Disturbed Peace,* about why I like being gay. Too often, in our attempt to communicate the pain of growing up gay, we forget to say that we also celebrate our homosexuality. This selection helps point that out. It's called "I Like It."

The young medical student finally blurted out the question which had been gnawing at him. "Do you ever regret being gay?"

"No," I said with a growing smile. "Sometimes I regret being so totally identified with my sexual orientation, but I never regret being gay."

"Wouldn't you really rather be straight?" asked one Jewish talk show host. "Would you rather be Christian?" I asked.

"Think of all the hostility you face," commented one black woman. "Because of that, wouldn't you prefer being heterosexual?"

"Who's telling who about hostility?" I queried. "How much would it take before you wished you were white?"

As supportive as they might become, many straight people have a lot of difficulty thinking of homosexuality as an intrinsic part of a person's psychological makeup. Even if they can be convinced that gay people didn't choose to be gay, they still need to hear us admit we would rather be like them.

I like being gay. I like knowing there is something very unique and even mysterious about me which separates me from most of the rest of the world. I like knowing that I share a special secret with a select group of men and women who lived before me and with those special few who will follow.

I like walking at life's edge as a pioneer; as an individual who must learn for himself the meaning of relationship, love of equals, sexuality and morality. Without the blessing of the Church and society, my life is one outrageous experiment after another. I like knowing that if I settle into a particular frame of thought, it is because I have found it appropriate and not because I was raised to believe that's the way things must be.

I like knowing that I can go anywhere in the world and meet someone who will smile that knowing smile which instantly says "Yes, I know; me too. Isn't it nice to not be alone? Hang in there." It is a twinkle and a smile which results not from being white or male or Catholic or American. It is a secret smile which only gay men and lesbians exchange.

I like exchanging that knowing smile with waiters in Galveston, flight attendants in Terre Haute, theater ushers in Detroit, salespeople in Boston and sunbathers in Sarasota. I like to give and receive those smiles at Mass, at lectures, in department stores, at the laundromat and on the street. I like the feeling I'm not alone.

I like believing the studies which indicate gay folk are generally smarter, more creative and more sensitive than non-gay folk. It makes me feel 'chosen.' I like knowing that a gay man's dinner party will usually be more artistic and that a gay disco will generally be more fun.

I like knowing that there is far less class division to be found at most gay parties. Janitors and lawyers and truck drivers and librarians are bound to unknowingly bump elbows.

I get a kick out of knowing that anti-gay people are probably wearing clothes designed by a gay person, living in a home decorated by a gay person, attending a play performed by a gay person and participating in a Sunday service celebrated by a gay person.

I laugh when I think of anti-gay men cheering gays on the football field and learning about other scores from a gay sportscaster. I especially love the thought of anti-gay Catholics praying to gay saints.

I like being gay for all of these and many more reasons. Primarily, though, I like being gay because it is an essential aspect of who I am . . . and I like myself (McNaught, 1981, pp. 122–123).

References

Bodo, Murray. *Francis: The journey and the dream.* Cincinnati: St. Anthony Messenger Press, 1972.

Hesse, Hermann. *Siddhartha.* New York: New Directions Publishing Corp., 1957.

McNaught, Brian. *A disturbed peace: Selected writings of an Irish Catholic homosexual.* Washington, D.C.: Dignity, Inc., 1981.

Chapter Two

GROWING UP LESBIAN AND CATHOLIC

Ann Borden

AS I write this, I must confess that I feel a great deal of anxiety. In this chapter I will share with you my own very personal feelings of pain, loneliness and isolation, confusion, fear, anger, love, joy and strength which stem from my recognition and eventual acceptance of myself as a lesbian woman. While it is usually threatening to communicate so personally with people one does not even know, my trepidation is heightened by the fact that I have not been able to reveal most of these feelings and experiences to my own parents.

I was born in Boston, fourth of six children in an Irish Catholic family. When I was about one year old, my family moved to Michigan where I grew up.

I am sort of your garden variety Catholic. I went to co-educational parochial schools for twelve years, did the normal, standard kinds of things, such as starting an anti-clique club in the eighth grade. I like to think that was my first involvement in social justice. But I think I felt very much outside of things and that was the way I was going to handle it. Five of us started the clandestine club, deciding that there should be more justice in the way our social milieu was structured. Although club membership was anonymous, the faculty cracked our code in two weeks and decided the club was certainly not in keeping with the general idea of Catholic education. Their initial idea to expel all of us was reversed, as such a move would have ruined the honor roll! That was one of my first conscious acts in aligning myself with groups concerned with social change. All that at the tender age of 13!

After graduation from grade school, I attended a parochial high school taught by the Sisters of Charity in Jackson, Michigan. I spent four years there getting involved with some of the inner-city racial issues which were hitting Michigan very, very hard in the late sixties. I started working at a racial center and began dating young black men from the public high school. (There were no black men in the Catholic high school.) This caused my parents a little anxiety. Trying to develop a sense of how I could be so privileged and how our society could exist the way it did, I began to think of how I, as a Catholic, was called upon to respond. Except for dating black men and trying to figure out some of the questions that had started to gnaw at me, high school was rather uneventful.

My first awareness that I might be a lesbian came about in a high school American literature class. We were reading Tennessee Williams, whose plays, of course, are populated with people of various sexual orientations. I found that fascinating; for me there was a resonance in these characters that was missing in much of the other literature I was reading. I pursued it as it excited a very deep curiosity in me that I really could not explain. I started reading other works with gay characters. I relished gay poets and gay literature, but very quietly. I never verbalized this to anyone. I simply kept reading and marking all the "weird" characters that paraded across the pages of literature. This identification with gay literary characters constituted my way of dealing with my lesbianism during high school years.

After high school graduation I decided that I wanted to attend a college outside Michigan. The only such college I knew was my mother's alma mater, Rosemont, outside of Philadelphia, so off I went! I had never been away from home nor in a single sex educational environment before. Because growing up in the Midwest is different from growing up on the East coast, I was not prepared for many of the cultural changes I would experience.

I spent my four college years editing the literary magazine, which published only poetry. It was difficult to edit a poetry magazine and I expended a great deal of energy on it.

I also became involved with the nascent feminist movement on campus. In retrospect I see that my comfort with being a lesbian increased in direct proportion with my comfort with being a woman during those four years. Being in a single sex environment was very good for me since it was the first time that I consciously thought of myself as a woman. I had thought of myself as a Catholic; I had thought of myself as a student, but I had never really thought of myself as female. This was strange because my mother was a very strong feminist although she never used the word. My mother objected very vocally to many things she experienced as a Catholic woman. Although I grew up with the idea that being a woman and being Catholic were both valid, I had never made distinctions in my own mind about who I was.

As many people fear, a single sex environment encourages same-sex experimentation. When I was a senior, a younger female student, who was experiencing much emotional turmoil, sensed my own sexual ambivalence and attempted what can only be described as a sort of awkward seduction. She compounded the situation by attempting to commit suicide immediately thereafter. Although I have a better grasp now of what was happening, I was absolutely shocked at the time. Even though I had had no physical same-sex experience, I had intellectually identified myself as a lesbian. I felt that this was who I was.

The recognition that I was in fact a lesbian hit me like a ton of bricks. I felt completely cut off from everything I had been before. I did not feel that I was female; I did not feel that I was Catholic; I did not feel I was a member of my own family. I felt as though I had a big scarlet "L" on my chest and that everybody could see it. I ran home. I flew home, rather, to Michigan and arrived at Metropolitan Airport, a real soggy mess. Although I was unable to say very much to my parents, I told them about the attempted suicide. I had apparently blubbered that previously over the phone because my mother surprisingly asked, "Oh, the woman didn't die? Well, what are you so upset about? What's going on?" I could not say to her "I'm coming to you materially different from the last time I saw you. I'm coming to you with the recognition that I have this identity that I don't know what to do with." I had wanted very much to lead my life as a Catholic woman but felt that this recognition now made it impossible.

I felt as though I had lost my identity. I believe that this feeling is a frequent one for gay people. The side effects of the recognition that we exist in isolation can be extremely devastating. This emotional upheaval, I believe, accounts in large part for much of the objectionable behavior in the homosexual community. If you believe that you exist in isolation and if you believe that you are beyond the Church and beyond the social fabric, then you can permit yourself to engage in all kinds of behaviors because you are an outlaw. I felt this for a time and I have spoken with many of my friends who think that there are no rules for them. They believe that whatever they want to do is valid because society has cut them off, their families have cut them off and their Church has cut them off. Therefore they can exist any way they want. One cannot continue like that for a long time without enduring a lot of psychic pain and without some hard questions about oneself in relation to humanity. You begin to wonder whether or not your actions really affect anybody and to question how valid you are as a human being. I do not intend to sound unnecessarily grim, but these are real concerns of anyone who has chosen to live outside the borders of society. To consciously affirm oneself as a lesbian or gay person means to live outside such socially acceptable borders.

After a brief stay at home which accomplished little in resolving my troubled state, I returned to Rosemont to complete my senior year. Although I considered professional counseling at one point, it was not financially feasible. It would also have been very difficult to justify to my parents and friends why I thought I needed counseling. The fact that I could not see a counselor became a very positive factor. After moping around for a couple of months, I shook myself and I said, "Wait a minute. if you had gone to bed with a man and after that experience called yourself a heterosexual, would you have felt the need to go to a therapist to find out why you were a heterosexual?"

"No," I answered myself. I reasoned that I was not in a position to afford therapy or analysis and I was not sure I needed it. I merely confirmed that my sexuality was that of a lesbian.

This reflection began something which was for me very helpful. I developed a way of looking at sexuality in the same way that I now look at intelligence. I believe that human beings can happen to fall anywhere on the spectrum of intelligence. There is nothing that is unnatural. There is a spectrum that runs from retardation to genius and perhaps far beyond in ways that we cannot measure. I believe the same thing is true of sexuality: being a lesbian or gay person is simply one notch on a spectrum of sexual experience, nothing more, nothing less.

What is upsetting to me is the fact that I had to come to this realization by myself. But perhaps in retrospect, I may not have been able to come to it in any other manner. By determining that I was not going to change my orientation, I experienced a kind of peace. Even so, I did not necessarily look forward to living my life as a lesbian, since I did not know what that entailed. Although the lack of understanding was nerve wracking, nonetheless, I determined that that was the way it was going to be.

For several months I put the whole issue on a back shelf. I needed to be concerned with getting a job and finding a place to live. After graduation I was still in no mood to return to Michigan. So six months later, after taking care of the details of employment and housing, I decided that I must deal with my sexual orientation. I knew that I was a lesbian but what did that mean?

I made some very deliberate moves. I had known a college woman I believed was gay; we had been friends. I sought out her company. We developed a friendship that was very good and a warmth that was very supportive. We eventually became lovers. I believe that was what I needed at the time. I felt renewed and affirmed. I felt there was a way that I could behave and love in a way that was acceptable.

So I did a very Catholic thing: I wrote my parents! I sent them a letter saying, "Dear parents, I just wanted you to know that I met someone I'm very fond of. We're developing a relationship and you'll be hearing a lot about her in my letters home, etc., etc." The next letter I received was from my mother. Now my mother is an avid bridge player; she plays duplicate bridge and is very good at it. She wrote, "Dear darling daughter, you are ruining my bridge game. I haven't been able to bid a single hand since I got your letter." I was extremely upset and mentally responded, "You don't know what I haven't been able to do." Her letter continued: she felt I was just going through a phase not unlike a phase that she herself had experienced thirty years earlier. She was sure that I would outgrow it and please not to talk to her about it anymore.

My father's response has always been very cryptic. He has never referred openly to the fact that he believes that I am a lesbian although the letter was intended for both my parents and I have reason to believe that they both read it. Several months after my telling letter, I informed my father that I was searching for a career. His advice was to join the Navy! I never asked him why he thought the Navy was particularly appropriate for me when he had never recommended it for any of his four sons! That is the way my parents dealt with my sexual orientation eight years ago. I have not spoken to my parents about my lesbianism since. Eight years is a long time. I do not believe they want to talk about it.

I have one brother in California who knows that I am gay. It was a hard fact for him to accept. When I first told him he responded that gay people are so superficial and irresponsible. Gay people do such annoying things, like public sex in the parks. I worked really hard to help him understand that that behavior did not describe me.

Over the years I have come to use the discussion of homosexuality as a funny kind of litmus test before I really get to know a person. I bring up the topic of homosexuality in conversation to determine how the person feels about it. If they pass that test and can discuss it with a fair amount of ease (if they do not shrink or cross their legs), then I should be able to speak with them a little more comfortably.

I gave this litmus test a couple years ago to my youngest brother who has been involved with the Word of God charismatic community in Ann Arbor for about six years. As we were talking about the Bible, I said, "Joe, what is sin?" Knowing the Bible far better than I, Joe was able to cite the chapters and verses in which sin had been defined in both the Old and the New Testaments. I pursued the conversation. "Joe, is production of nuclear weapons a sin?"

"No," laconically.

"Why not?" I pressed.

"There just isn't anything in the Bible that talks about nuclear weapons."

"I know there's nothing in the Bible. There are a lot of things that aren't in the Bible. So how do you reconcile those things?"

Joe had never seriously considered this kind of reasoning.

"What about homosexuality?" I continued.

"That's a sin." It seemed obvious to my brother. Why? Because it was in the Bible. There are proscriptions in the Old Testament and in the Pauline epistles on the subject.

I find it difficult to express precisely how the entire encounter affected me. I will never be able to speak from my heart freely to Joe as long as he remains in that community which interprets the Bible literally. I will never be able to ask him to look at me as his sister, as a Catholic, and as a woman who thinks and feels very deeply about her faith and who wants very much to belong to her church as he can belong. I fear that, if I try to share my personal convictions about homosexuality with him, there will be an iron wall raised between us that I don't have the resources to go around or under or above.

I am not yet ready to undertake the major, arduous and lengthy project of educating my parents and my other brothers and sisters about the myths and the realities of lesbianism and male homosexuality. I have a very comfortable relationship with each of them. I believe they see me as a two dimensional person. I feel that my parents and other siblings do not think that I have grown up fully as a sexual adult. They do not know that I have been in a relationship for seven years that to me approximates a marriage.

At this time my primary relationship is experiencing some difficulty. About two months ago, my lover and I separated. We are currently seeing a counselor to try to patch up what was for us at one time a very good thing.

These personal struggles go on and my involvement with Dignity goes on. My talks on radio stations, my appearances on television shows and even this chapter goes on without any of my family being aware of them. This is very difficult for me. I do not believe that my own or anyone's sexuality should be displayed. Rather, sexuality should be integrated into our lives. I occasionally feel that I am a diminished person because I am not able to do this.

As I recounted above, my feminism developed while I was in college. After graduation, my feminist instincts precipitated my difficulties with the church. I was going to church on Sundays. In Philadelphia, Sunday Mass is a form of torture! Philadelphia parishes are very closed, structured communities that are antithetical to what I experienced growing up in Michigan and later while attending college. There was little relevance in what I heard coming from the altar. There was very little sense of belonging. There was very little that was required of me in order to assert my membership. But what was required of me was absolutely impossible for me to give because it meant being a kind of woman that I could not be. I did not have children. I did not have a husband. Birth control was not something that had to be emphatically stressed in my relationship to God. I was just generally having a difficult time as a woman in the Catholic Church.

I decided to stop being a Catholic because I was getting absolutely nothing from this relationship. For me, to stop being a Catholic, I thought, meant simply to stop going to Mass. But I found that I could not stop being a Catholic. By that time, being a Catholic had gotten into my fiber in a strange way. Upon analysis, I found that I really liked being a Catholic. My way of looking at the world and the values that I held came about as a result of being Catholic. I did not want to discard those values or that vision, nor could I. What I had to do was construct a way of being Catholic that was satisfying to me. This is treacherous for people because they start reinventing the Church. That is exactly what I have done. I have come up with all sorts of definitions for words like marriage, sin, chastity and celibacy that have nothing to do with conventional meanings as those words are understood by the Catholic Church. I had to come to that because I was doing things that felt emotionally and spiritually correct and which I believed were consistent with what I knew of Jesus Christ and of the underpinning of my faith. However, I found that my actions were at variance with what I was told I was permitted to do. Of necessity I had to redefine many concepts.

I was in a relationship for seven years that is as close to a marriage as I have ever come. I never fully realized that I was in a marriage until I committed adultery. I had to acknowledge that I deliberately transgressed the commitment I had expressed. I had done it in a sexual way and to me that was adultery. When I decided to redefine this relationship in ways acceptable to me, I had to really question the meaning of divorce. How can there be a divorce if there is no marriage? Yet, I felt as though I was going through a divorce process. I had lived with someone, shared a life with someone and tried very earnestly to make that as complete as I could. When it ended, what else could it be for a Catholic but a divorce? Yet in the eyes of many people, what I was doing by leaving the situation was preferable to staying in it. I was getting strange messages that to live as a free sexual agent is preferable to living as a committed sexual adult in a partner relationship.

At times I believe that we must define what we mean when we say that we are members of the Catholic Church. What do we mean when we say that we believe a whole list of things uttered early in the Mass? I have had to become a "pick and choose" Catholic primarily as a woman and secondarily as a lesbian.

About five years ago a friend of mine introduced me to Dignity. I was having a very traumatic Lent. I was going to Mass and trying to recapture the sense of closeness to God that I had felt when I was a lot younger. But I did not seem to be feeling closer to God. A friend discovered Dignity and dropped me off at a service. I walked in. In a tiny apartment were twelve men. About five of them had physical handicaps. There were no women and they were celebrating mass on top of a television set. I felt quite uncomfortable on one level because there were no women and because I felt that I was in the presence of people who were sexually handicapped as was I, but who were also physically handicapped. So there were the outward reminders that we were very wounded people who were gathering together to say Mass. But despite this, I felt such a sense of warmth and belonging.

In some ways it was the same warmth I felt when I first went into a gay bar when I was 19. It looked very natural to see women dancing together and that is how I felt at this eucharist. It was very natural. There was a real sense of what we are supposed to be doing when we celebrate liturgy together; sharing—sharing all the parts of ourselves, not just the acceptable ones or the public aspects.

That chapter has since grown to about 120 people. Mass each Sunday is celebrated in an Episcopal parish house because we cannot meet in Philadelphia in a Catholic church. About 200 people participate at Mass each week—about 96 percent of whom are men.

I wish to comment on this phenomenon of Dignity as a predominantly male experience. After I heard John McNeill speak in 1976 on a lecture tour after publication of his book, *The Church and the Homosexual,* I began to consider what was really so terrible about being a homosexual person. I came to the conclusion that the real crime of being a homosexual is the crime of being non-male. It seems that our institution has defined everything in relation to the norm and that norm is male. I exist in the eyes of the Church not as a woman but as a non-male. Similarly, gay persons exist in the eyes of the Church as non-males, engaged in behavior that does not dignify them as males. I am still in the Church because I am fighting very hard for inclusion as a non-male. In other words, I want to be regarded on my own merits as a woman and as a lesbian.

Dignity has a difficult time attracting women, I believe, because many lesbians have experienced a dual sense of rejection. By virtue of being female they are already beyond consideration of the Catholic Church. They are second class citizens. By being sexual people who express their sexuality in a very particular way the Church has no use for them. Any woman who has tried to fathom the enigma of a sexless Mary, the mother of God, has encountered this problem because she comes to realize that when a woman expresses her sexuality, she is knocked from atop her pedestal. A woman cannot aspire to become the kind of person that she feels called to be. For a lesbian this is particularly difficult. For a woman to admit to herself, "I've been kicked in the pants because I'm a woman and I've been kicked in the pants because I'm a lesbian yet I still feel some kind of identification with my oppressor," requires a very convoluted way of looking at the world.

For many women it is much easier to develop a goddess-worshipping community or a community based on an alternative spirituality rather than to align themselves continually with an organization that rejects them. But I am still a Catholic because I believe that to limit the Church to such a narrow vision is an affront to Christ. I simply do not believe that we have been barred by Christ from participating fully in the institution that was founded in his name.

I usually present a very calm demeanor to the world. I work in a bank—an ordinary job. Although I live an ordinary life, I live far beyond conventional expectations. The parts of me that are most essential are not expressed or publicly known. This is devastating to many people, especially if they are unable to find, as I have found, a real community. I have found this community in Dignity. Dignity is composed of people who support me and believe that I am a valid member of the human race and a valid member of the Roman Catholic Church. However, most lesbians or gay people, I would say, are existing in some sort of psychic isolation, sharing their true selves with a few close friends and, in some cases, with their families.

I am very happy that I am a lesbian woman. I would not trade it for anything in the world because I have learned things through my lesbianism as well as through other facets of my life that I probably could not have learned in any other way. An extremely fortunate woman, I have been given numerous gifts from God, one of which has been my sexuality and another my Catholicism.

I am pleased by this opportunity to communicate my life's most significant moments to you. I firmly believe that we need to challenge our church to listen more sensitively to the experiences of other Catholics who have grown up as lesbian or gay. It is in this appreciative and inviting spirit that I have shared my journey with you.

Chapter Three

NEW SOCIOLOGICAL THEORY ON HOMOSEXUALITY

Jeannine Gramick

BY way of preface to this chapter, it is necessary to note that it operates on the assumption that various branches of the social sciences, such as psychology, psychiatry, anthropology, biology and sociology, must inform and contribute to a meaningful reflection on the complicated ethical questions in contemporary society. It is appropriate then that this book on homosexuality began with chapters on the lived experience of lesbian and gay persons themselves. A concern for the person in her or his existential context and social structure demands an interdisciplinary approach to Christian morality.

The moral theologian Robert Springer (1968) noted that "the opening to behavioral science as a source of ethical values was dictated by Vatican II (p. 55)."* To suggest that sociology impacts ethical analysis does not imply a surrender of, nor an attack on, traditional values or official teachings. Rather, a thorough grounding in sociological theory and fact enables the ethicist to determine the applicability of these values and teachings for different cultural and social situations.

The main task of the social and behavioral sciences is to collect and analyze the data of human experience. The theologian then uses the sociological analysis as

* See references at close of chapter.

input for building an ethical framework from which to evaluate human behavior. Milhaven (1970) goes so far as to claim that "for contemporary ethics the use of the behavioral sciences *is* morality (p. 125)." Malloy (1980) interprets him to mean that "when the best wisdom of a social science has been ascertained, we have grounds for assurance that moral judgments based on this consensus are in tune with reality (p. 127)."

The importance of the social sciences in contributing insights for theology has not always been recognized. It is a sad indictment of Christian theology that in the introduction to his book, *Homosexuality and the Western Christian Tradition,* Derrick Sherwin Bailey (1955), a prominent Anglican moralist, found it necessary to note: "I have not carried this general account beyond the end of the Middle Ages because it does not appear that the tradition has undergone any significant alteration since that time—although various legal and other modifications have occurred which have affected judicial practice and, to a limited extent, public opinion (p. viii)." Despite significant social reorganization regarding the issue of homosexuality between the Middle Ages and the mid-twentieth century, the official Christian churches had not reexamined their understanding of the morality of homosexual behavior.

There is a plurality of theories in every social science, some of which have been used to explain the phenomenon of homosexuality. During the first half of the twentieth century, a psychiatric theory to describe homosexuality was widely held among professionals. According to this "medical model" or psychoanalytic model, homosexuality was a "neurotic distortion of the total personality (Bergler, 1957, p. 9)."

This view of homosexuality is affirmed by Ellis (1956) who asserts that "confirmed homosexuals are, on the whole, exceptionally disturbed individuals (p. 194)." The work of Bieber (1962) in his study of 106 male homosexuals illustrated the problem in the research of this school of psychiatrists. Bieber's sample is composed of patients from his therapeutic practice. These researchers concluded that their patient subjects verified their assumption that adult homosexuality is psychopathologic.

These pseudo-scientific studies based on skewed populations have been damaging to the group under consideration. While the literature of such clinicians has been soundly criticized by the academic community, their ideological fallacies have been popularly espoused and the consequent harm on a personal level cannot be overlooked.

In 1973, the board of trustees of the American Psychiatric Association, the traditional archenemy of the homosexual person, revised its diagnosis of homosexuality. No longer was a homosexual orientation considered a mental disorder. In its diagnostic manual, the APA created a new category, "sexual orientation disturbance," for those homosexual individuals not well-adjusted to their sexual orientation. To settle charges that the APA board decision regarding a psychiatric reclassification of homosexuality resulted from political pressure and lobbying from militant gay organizations, a referendum of the Association was conducted in the spring of 1974. More than 10,000 psychiatrists, or 58 percent of those responding to the poll, concurred with the decision of the board. A 1977 survey by the American Medical Association claimed to discredit the APA referendum by reporting that the majority of the psychiatrists responding to its survey maintained that homosexuality was a pathological adaptation to normal sexual development. However, its 25 percent response represented little more than 1,000 psychiatrists in contrast to the 10,000 psychiatrists of the APA referendum.

The American Psychological Association soon followed suit to declassify homosexuality from the category of disorder or sickness. Naturally, it is not to be inferred that *all* psychiatrists or *all* psychologists concur with the postures articulated officially by their ruling bodies, no more so than that all Catholics concur with the pronouncements made by their official hierarchies.

The trend among professional sexologists seems to view homosexual behavior not as a sexual deviation but rather as a sexual variation. In altering the language used to conceptualize this phenomenon, not only in professional journals but also in college textbooks on human sexuality, psychology or sociology, the social scientist must not be ignorant of the vital role she or he plays in modifying the current societal reaction to homosexuality. The language and categories employed to deal with social constructs cannot be divorced from meanings and emotional content. Linguistic analysis testifies to the contributing role of language in shaping, reinforcing or modifying attitudes. For example, the displacement of such rhetoric as "deaf and dumb" to describe those audially and aphonically impaired helps to assuage the colloquial imputations of stupidity. Hence, the trend to regard homosexual activity as a variant, rather than a deviant, form of sexual expression undoubtedly initiates as well as reflects attitudinal change in dealing with the issue.

In the latter part of the twentieth century, the "sickness theory" of psychoanalysis has fallen into disfavor as an approach to homosexuality. Social researchers have begun to examine homosexuality from a different perspective: the perspective of symbolic interactionism. Just what precisely *is* symbolic interactionism? And how can homosexuality be understood from this viewpoint? I shall explore each of these questions in turn.

1. *What is Symbolic Interactionism?*

During the first few decades of the twentieth century, symbolic interactionism developed, largely unnoticed, around Chicago. It has now become a forceful perspective on which many sociological studies are based (Blumer, 1969; Petras and Meltzer, 1973; Plummer, 1975). In setting a direction and method for the symbolic interactionist framework, Herbert Blumer (1969) postulates three statements: 1) humans act on the basis of *meanings,* 2) such meanings flow from *social interactions* with other human beings, and 3) such meanings are altered through a *process* of interpretation.

A. *Meaning:* It is precisely symbolic meanings which distinguish the human from the non-human world. Meanings do not inherently abide within objects but rather arise from the interpretive process of individuals constantly in dialogue with other individuals. As the empirical world emerges from a state of flux, meanings are continually modified and reconstructed.

Plummer (1975) graphically illustrates this first postulate concerning meaning by an example. Sexual meanings, he maintains, are not attached to certain behaviors in and of themselves.

> The 'mind' has to define something as 'sexual' before it is sexual in its consequences. As a simple illustration of this, two extreme cases may be cited: the first involves a woman lying naked while a man fingers her vagina, the second involves a boy watching a football match. If one was asked as an external observer to define which situation was sexual—by 'universalist, commonsense' definitions—there would be little to query. The first was sexual, the second was not. However, if one ignored the purely behavioral aspects and focused upon the meanings that the actors give to the situation, quite a different picture may emerge. For the man fingering the woman may be shown to be a doctor involved in a vaginal examination; and both actors may have produced clear definitions of the situation as being a medical one (Emerson, 1970; Henslin and Biggs, 1971); while the boy watching the football match may be busily involved in defining the boys playing football as sexual objects, imagining them in sexual acts, and interpreting internal sensations as sexual ones (pp. 30–31).

B. *Social Interaction:* The study of group differences, for example, must incorporate an analysis of the characteristics of those deemed different. But the concept of group differences cannot be comprehended in isolation from the persons of the majority group who define various people as different and, in consequence, react in a stigmatizing or prejudicial manner. Within a symbolic interactionist analysis, the critical variable of societal reactions cannot be neglected. Becker (1963) believes that consideration of reactions and interactions are crucial. He says, "Social groups create deviance by making the rules whose infraction constitutes deviance, and by applying those rules to particular people and labelling them as outsiders (p. 9)."

Action, reaction and interaction regarding sexual difference is associated with varying tolerance levels. Ford and Beach (1951) have established the existence of differing levels of tolerance toward sexual diversification across cultures. Within any given culture, small community centers, with their closed groupings where any difference is frowned upon, exhibit less toleration for sexual differences than large urban areas where those deviating from various norms may gather with each other in virtual anonymity for mutual support. Similarly, tolerance levels within variegated groups tend to be higher than those with more homogeneous clusters.

In addition to various levels of toleration, the nature of one's conception of sexual differences plays a large role in societal reaction. Such conceptions, often ill-founded and undocumented, are frequently generated by stereotypes, legends or mythical traditions by which society comes to associate certain characteristics with a given group. For example, rapists are commonly imagined to be Negro males who vent sexual violence on unsuspecting white women in a dimly lit alley (Amir, 1971) or male homosexuals are considered child molesting, promiscuous, effeminate perverts (Hoffman, 1968). Although researchers establish that such misconceptions may in fact be true of some members in the group in question, such generalizations to describe the entire group cannot adequately be asserted. Yet such stereotypes persist in popular opinion and provide a foundation for action by societal agents of control.

C. *Process:* Process analysis forms the cornerstone of an interactionist approach. Shur (1969) writes, "The societal reaction conception is pre-eminently a dynamic one. It insists that deviant behavior can be understood only in terms of constantly changing states reflecting complex interaction processes, that it is quite misleading to treat it as a static condition (p. 310)."

Instead of accounting for minority behavior in terms of static constructions or predetermined conditions, such as dysfunction in the social or family structure, the interactionist formulates not a simple cause-effect model, but a more complex cumulative-cause prototype delineating the sequential processes involved. Since the commitment to minority behavior is not an "all at once" situation, the symbolic interactionist focuses on these processes through which one becomes different.

Within the past two decades the theory of symbolic interactionism has evolved from a position of being a virtual "lone voice in the wilderness" made audible by a few revolutionary academicians to the novel status of sociological orthodoxy. As any established theory or structure will rightly be critiqued, symbolic interactionism has not escaped scholarly examination. But far from being a fad the interactionist perspective is well-grounded in intellectual positions and has produced a rich quality of research.

2. *How Can Homosexuality Be Understood from the Perspective of Symbolic Interactionism?*

From this brief explanation of symbolic interactionism, I now turn to the second question of how homosexuality can be understood within this interactionist framework. I shall consider the three main tenets of symbolic interactionism and apply them to the specific issue of homosexuality.

A. *Homosexuality and Meaning:* Until recently most research on homosexuality has investigated why and how some persons transgress societal sexual norms which are assumed to form part of an absolute reality that exists without reference to personal meanings. In the last two decades the assumption of such an absolute reality has been challenged not only by interactionists but also by phenomenologists. Reality is not viewed as an absolute but as located in consciousness and as a consequence of specific interactions. Homosexuality then assumes various meanings dependent upon the situation and the individuals involved.

Only when one admits of the variety of subjective meanings which can be attached to identical sexual behavior, can the question, "What constitutes sexual deviancy or normality?" be posed. Berger (1966) has put the matter this way: "Sexual roles are constructed within the same general precariousness that marks the entire social fabric. Cross-cultural comparisons of sexual conduct bring home to us the near-infinite flexibility that men [sic] are capable of in organizing their lives in this area. What is normality and maturity in one culture is pathology and regression in another (p. 180)."

Empirical research into the content of homosexual meanings is sorely lacking. Virtually nonexistent are studies to determine how homosexual meanings are formed, translated, interpreted and made orthodox in a given cultural setting. How is it that a particular agent includes certain instances of sexual deviance within the scope of his or her definition and not others? Gagnon and Simon (1968) have rightly observed, "There is no form of sexual activity that is not deviant at some time, in some social location, in some specified relationships, or with some partners (p. 107)."

So while the clinician approaches homosexuality as an entity possessing objective attributes to be explained and described, the interactionist sees the conventional categorization of homosexuality as a problem to be explored in itself. Sexual differences then, and their meanings and definitions, have a socially constructed nature.

The meaning assigned to homosexuality must of necessity be viewed in social contexts. In many cultures not expressly dominated by the Judeo-Christian ethic, homosexuality has not always been denounced as sharply. Ford and Beach (1951) documented that, in 64 percent of the non-industrialized cultures studied, homosexuality had socially acceptable meanings. Westermarck (1917) and de Becker (1967) present historical evidence that homosexuality has been tolerated if not approved in numerous societies throughout history. While it is controverted that these studies validate homosexuality, at the very least they indicated that homosexuality may be invested with a range of subjective meanings from total acceptance to neutral indifference to vitriol.

The symbolic interactionist, then, questions the meanings of homosexuality as a sin, a sickness, a crime, an abnormality, by revealing the highly subjective nature of such conceptions. Through social construction subjective meanings have become objectified into a truth or order of nature. The interactionist unmasks this "absolute" reality for a subjective and relativized world in which meanings are always diverse and often problematic.

B. *Homosexuality and Social Interaction:* The second major tenet of symbolic interactionism is that meanings flow from social interactions with other human beings. Of major importance in an interactionist analysis is the study of homosexuality in relation to the societal reactions which often stigmatize it as deviance. What is needed is a systematic study of the ways in which individuals and groups apprehend and respond to lesbian and gay people instead of a concentration on the characteristics of the homosexually oriented person as if such an analysis were possible without reference to societal contexts. Data are needed on how homosexuality is approached by teachers, parents, the churches, the media and other control agents.

Sociological research on homosexuality has focused on the subject of homophobia with increasing frequency since the early 1970s. Homophobia can be defined as any systemic judgment which advocates negative myths and stereotypes about lesbian or gay persons. It is any structured belief which does not equate the value of same-sex lifestyles and opposite-sex lifestyles. Churchill (1967) maintained that sex-negative cultures attempted to repress homosexual people and same-sex behavior through the process of socialization. He describes contemporary American culture as exercising negative social judgment upon all sexual behavior outside of the Judeo-Christian tradition. He further states that prejudice against homosexuality in others is merely an exaggeration of attitudes regarding most other aspects of sexual life. In other words, according to Churchill, the sex-negative individual represses or suppresses his or her own sexuality and seeks to restrain the sexual practices of others. On the other hand, the sex-positive individual is accepting of her or his own sexuality and, consequently, accepting of the sexuality, behavior and values of others.

According to some studies a basic component of homophobia is the need to preserve a double standard between men and women. MacDonald, Huggins, Young and Swanson (1973) have found that advocacy of traditional sex roles correlates highly with hostility toward lesbian and gay people. Their investigation tested the different explanations offered by two hypotheses about the sources of negative attitudes toward homosexuality. They postulate that attitudes are determined by conservative standards of sexual morality and by a need to preserve a double standard. That is, some people condemn the lesbian or gay person who manifests inappropriate gender characteristics in order to reduce sex-role confusion. From the MacDonald study it appears that attitudes toward lesbian women and gay men are more highly associated with a support for a double standard for the sexes than with permissive or nonpermissive attitudes regarding premarital sexual intimacy.

Morin and Wallace (1976) found that the best predictor of homophobic attitudes is a belief in the traditional family power structure, i.e., a dominant father, submissive mother and obedient children. The second best predictor of homophobia was advocacy of traditional attitudes toward women. In addition, traditional religious beliefs were predictive of both traditional beliefs about women and negative attitudes toward homosexuality. These studies support Churchill's (1967) theory that socialization concerning appropriate roles for women and men is an impetus which influences fear, dread, and hatred of lesbian and gay people.

Homophobia has also been defined as an "irrational fear or intolerance of homosexuality" (Lehne, 1976) or as "an irrational, persistent, fear or dread of homosexuals" (MacDonald, 1976). This approach views homophobia more as a personal, intrinsic condition rather than as a cultural belief.

Studies have confirmed that people who are more negative in their attitudes toward homosexuality have been found to be more authoritarian (MacDonald, 1974; Smith, 1971), more dogmatic (Hood, 1973), more status conscious (Smith, 1971), more sexually rigid (Berry & Marks, 1969; Brown & Amoroso, 1975; Dunbar, Brown & Amoroso, 1973; Dunbar, Brown and Vourinen, 1973; Smith, 1971), more guilty and negative about their own sexual impulses (Berry & Marks, 1969; Dunbar, Brown & Amoroso, 1973). The above data seem to imply that people who are prejudiced against lesbian or gay people tend to be prejudiced against any persons or views which differ from their own opinions or that they tend to be sexually conservative.

Attitudes toward homosexuality and toward lesbian and gay persons have also been studied not only from a cultural and personal perspective but also from the standpoint of gender, occupation, age, socioeconomic background and geographic location. The question of whether men or women in our society are more homophobic has received much attention recently in almost all of the attitudinal studies conducted. Although homophobia is found both in men and women, males seem to be more threatened by homosexuality than females (Brown & Amoroso, 1975). One explanation may be that male homosexuality is viewed in the American culture as being much more in opposition to socially stereotypical sex roles than is lesbianism. Gay men are thus more vulnerable to social censure and repression than are lesbian women. Society's legal prosecution and harassment of gay men and the relative absence of such legal repression toward lesbian women seem to support this theory. Feminist analysis of the inequitable values assigned to male and female roles in American society likewise implies that the lack of conformity to the male sex role is a more serious societal violation than breaking with traditional female role expectations. Lesbians are thus judged less harshly because they are perceived to be aspiring to a male and therefore more valued role. On the other hand, attitudes toward gay men are more severe since they are perceived to be mimicking an inferior and, from a male perspective, a more degrading role.

Occupation, socioeconomic background, age and geographic location, have not been found to have any great significance in determining the causes of homophobia. One, however, which several writers (Smith, 1971; Nyberg and Alston, 1976–1977) stress ought to be given more attention in the area of research on homophobia is religion.

C. *Homosexuality and Process:* The third major tenet of symbolic interactionism postulates that meanings are altered through a continual process of interpretation. To gain insight into the entire process of becoming sexually different, an understanding of the process of sexual contextualization is needed. From the perspective of the symbolic interactionist, human beings with various biological and physiological capacities to respond to sexual stimuli are born into a culturally created "natural" or "objective" world containing sexual meanings. The process of becoming sexual is an unconsciously learned procedure subject to certain biological constraints. Together with metaphysical meanings from an objective reality, sexual intentions are developed and interpreted in action and interaction with significant others. Plummer (1975) refers to the administration over time of these sexual meanings as an "erotic career (p. 57)." Because of the development of attachments, commitments and worldviews, sexual orientation may become stabilized.

For most individuals adolescence is a critical period of time during which sexual meanings are formed. But the termination of adolescence does not signal the cessation of the process of becoming sexual. Sexual socialization spans the whole life experience.

There are theoretical reasons, and some empirical research, to assert the existence of considerable sexual variation on the private and personal level. The wide range of variation includes the asexual individual who has successfully obliterated any traces of sexual fantasies, desires, or behaviors from his or her lifestyle as well as the most sexually active prostitute. Subject to biological constraints, the process of learning to be sexual is intricate and provides substantive areas for future research.

Static portraits of homosexuality do not fit into an interactionist theory. The interactionist views the sources of homosexuality as part of an ongoing sequential process. Becoming gay or lesbian is not a sudden gambol from one static state to another but a process characterized by ordered stages.

In a 1980 study of coming out among lesbian women conducted by New Ways Ministry, it was found that self-acknowledgment of a lesbian identity is preceded by a series of ordered stages. Gradually, through interaction with peers, adults and the social milieu, the young female begins to sense a feeling of "being different." Though she may cognitively understand the meaning of homosexuality, she does not yet attribute homosexual meaning to the initial clue of "feeling different." In adolescence her physical/erotic attractions become more manifest. Eventually she meets known lesbian women. At this point, those factors which are more specifically sexual in nature come into play and directly influence a lesbian self-conception. That is, genital behavior and establishing a physical relationship with another woman directly contribute to her thinking of herself as a lesbian. However, usually many years of increasing suspicions coupled with denial and repression pass before a woman is ready to make a lesbian declaration. The study confirmed the theory that developing a lesbian identity is achieved through a process of social interactions.

Conclusion: In the introductory remarks, I postulated the thesis that the social sciences contribute necessary, though not sufficient, data to theological reflection. Having developed a description of the sociological perspective of symbolic interactionism and having situated homosexuality within this theory, we may now logically ask, "What implications does a symbolic interactionist approach to homosexuality have for theological development?"

First, the Christian churches seemed eager to embrace the medical model of homosexuality which assigned the meaning of sick or abnormal to the phenomenon of homosexuality. Such a meaning appeared gratuitously to exonerate or diminish the guilt associated with same-sex activity. But the medical model illustrated by studies lacking random samples or matched control groups has been severely critiqued and rejected by the academic community precisely because of the inadequate research designs. With increasing frequency homosexuality is viewed by sexual researchers as a variant form of sexual behavior. It would seem that the moral theologian, then, must re-examine the traditional contention that homosexual acts are "unnatural" and attempt to reconcile, if possible, such a meaning of homosexuality with current sociological thought. Further, the churches have traditionally assigned the meaning of "sin" to homosexual behavior, if not to the homosexual orientation. If all sin against God and against human beings is rooted in some universal moral law, and if some cultures exist in which homosexual behavior not only is considered "not sinful" but also is invested with social prestige, how can the ethicist assert that homosexual behavior violates some universal moral law?

Secondly, homosexual people cannot be understood in isolation from the reactions and interactions with the dominant heterosexual group which defines them as sick, sinful, criminal, or abnormal. Because of this fact, the theologian must, of necessity, focus on the defining control group to determine whether or not discriminatory or prejudicial (i.e. objectively immoral) coping strategies are being employed. The moral theologian, then, must devote attention to the social sin of a lack of a proper respect for individual human differences.

Finally, if the social sciences contribute to an understanding of becoming constitutionally homosexual as a gradual process which is rooted in prenatal factors which become central to the personality structure as increasingly thought (Bell, Weinberg and Hammersmith, 1981), what implications does that hold for the freedom of the individual to act contrary to her or his natural development? The direction of current sociological theory and research seems to challenge the moral theologian to reassess the ancient answers and to formulate more enlightened questions on homosexuality.

References

Amir, M. *Patterns in forcible rape.* Chicago: University of Chicago Press, 1971.

Bailey, D. S. *Homosexuality and the western christian tradition.* London: Longmans, Green, 1955.

Becker, H. S. *Outsiders: Studies in the sociology of deviance.* London: Macmillan, 1963.

Bell, A. P., Weinberg, M. S., & Hammersmith, S. K. *Sexual preference: Its development in men and women.* Bloomington: Indiana University Press, 1981.

Berger, P. L. *Invitation to sociology: A humanistic perspective.* Harmondsworth: Penguin Books, 1966.

Bergler, E. *Homosexuality: Disease or way of life.* New York: Hill and Wang, 1957.

Berry, D. F., & Marks, P. A. Antihomosexual prejudice as a function of attitude toward own sexuality. *APA Proceedings,* 1969, 4, 573–574.

Bieber, I. *et al. Homosexuality: A psychoanalytic study.* New York: Basic Books, 1962.

Blumer, H. *Symbolic interactionism: Perspective and method.* New Jersey: Prentice-Hall, 1969.

Brown, M. & Amoroso, D. M. Attitudes toward homosexuality among West Indian male and female college students. *Journal of Social Psychology,* 1975, 97, 163–168.

Churchill, W. *Homosexual behavior among males: A cross-cultural and cross-species investigation.* New York: Hawthorne, 1967.

deBecker, R. *The other face of homosexuality: The definitive study of homosexuality.* London: Neville Spearman, 1967.

Dunbar, J., Brown, M. & Amoroso, D. M. Some correlates of attitudes toward homosexuality. *Journal of Social Psychology,* 1973, 89, 271–279.

Dunbar, J., Brown, M. & Vourinen, S. Attitude toward homosexuality among Brazilian and Canadian college students. *Journal of Social Psychology,* 1973, 90, 173–183.

Ellis, A. The effectiveness of psychotherapy with individuals who have severe homosexual problems. *Journal of Consulting Psychology,* 1956, 20, 191–195.

Ford, C. S. & Beach, F. *Patterns of sexual behavior.* New York: Harper and Row, 1951.

Gagnon, J. H. & Simon, W. S. Sexual deviance in contemporary America. *Annals of the American Academy of Political and Social Science,* 1968, 376, 107–122.

Hoffman, M. *The gay world.* New York: Basic Books, 1968.

Hood, R. W. Dogmatism and opinions about mental illness. *Psychological Reports,* 1973, 32, 1283–1290.

Lehne, G. K. Homophobia among men. In D. David and R. Brannon (Eds.), *The forty-nine percent majority: The male sex role.* New York: Addison-Wesley, 1976.

MacDonald, A. P. Homophobia: Its roots and meanings. *Homosexual Counseling Journal,* 1976, 3, 23–33.

MacDonald, A. P. The importance of sex-role to gay liberation. *Homosexual Counseling Journal,* 1974, 1, 169–180.

MacDonald, A. P., Jr., Huggins, J., Young, S. & Swanson, R. A. Attitudes toward homosexuality: Preservation of sex morality or the double standard? *Journal of Consulting and Clinical Psychology,* 1973, 40, 161.

Malloy, E. A. Homosexual way of life: Methodological considerations in the use of sociological considerations in christian ethics. *Catholic Theological Society of America Proceedings,* June, 1979, 34, 123-140.

Milhaven, J. G. *Toward a new catholic morality.* Garden City: Doubleday, 1970.

Morin, S. F. & Wallace, S. Traditional values, sex-role stereotyping, and attitudes toward homosexuality. Paper presented at the meeting of the Western Psychological Association, Los Angeles, April 1976.

Nyberg, K. L. & Alston, J. P. Analysis of public attitudes toward homosexual behavior. *Journal of Homosexuality,* 1976-1977, 2, 99-107.

Petras, J. W. & Meltzer, B. Theoretical and ideological variations in contemporary interactionism. *Catalyst,* 1973, 7, 1-8.

Plummer, K. *Sexual stigma: An interactionist account.* London: Routledge & Kegan Paul, 1975.

Schur, E. M. Reactions to deviance: A critical assessment. *American Journal of Sociology,* 1969, 75, 309.

Smith, K. T. Homophobia: A tentative personality profile. *Psychological Reports,* 1971, 29, 1091-1094.

Springer, R. Conscience, behavioral science and absolutes. In C. Curran (Ed.), *Absolutes in moral theology?* Washington: Corpus, 1968.

Westermarck, E. Origins and development of the moral ideas. Vol. 2. London: Macmillan, 1917.

Chapter Four

OVERCOMING THE STRUCTURED EVIL OF MALE DOMINATION AND HETEROSEXISM

Barbara Zanotti

A POET mused, "I dream of that day when my child will say to me, 'Mother, what was war?'" I will never hear those words from my own four children. They live in a world where war is a habit of mind, where weapons acquisition is an end in itself, and where the ultimate weapon is the longed-for Holy Grail.

The religion of nuclear theology is all too clear—idolatry of the bomb. This new religion posits faith in the use of fear; force as the ground of international relations, and trust in the technological imperative. Its beliefs involve doctrines of counterforce, rough parity, flexible response and mutually assured destruction. It speaks of surrender to the creed of acceptable losses and winnable nuclear war (Lifton, 1979).

This is the context within which we live: an insane collision course of power and annihilation. In this chapter I wish to examine 1) the dreadful roots of this pathological ethos, 2) the results of structured male dominance on sexuality, 3) the contribution of lesbian and gay persons toward eliminating the evils of misogyny, and 4) the life-giving fruits of feminism.

First, what are the roots of this pathological religion of nuclear destruction in which humanity is engulfed at this point in history? To answer this all important question we must delve deeply into the very foundations of our society, for the making of war is not separate from the culture from which it stems. I want to turn our attention to social arrangements which contain and predict the savagery of war, and within this framework to weave together the specific concerns of this book.

We live within an economic policy based on maximization of profit and within an order which requires the support of other systemic forces, among which is structured male supremacy. It is essential to understand the nature of patriarchal organization and the determining role of this paradigm in every aspect of our lives.

Male dominance, i.e., rule by elite males, is a legacy of power passed on from father to son which provides access and privilege of varying amounts to the male gender class. Across the institutions, men are the appointed leaders; women, the designated followers. Men and male-identified values of competition, aggression and might are assigned to the public order; while women and so-called feminine virtues of compassion, gentleness, and nurturance are relegated to the private realm. Thus stated, the male disposition becomes the value center of the culture. A double ethic obtains: loving nurturance in the home and disembodied rationality in the public sphere (Miller, 1976; Ruether, 1975).

Within this scheme, certain dualisms obtain. He is spirit. She is flesh. He is thought. She is feeling. He is heaven. She is earth. He is mind. She is body. The dreadful consequences of this split, diminishing women and men alike, are all around us and within us. An unconscious ideology preserves the illusion that this is the natural order of existence. Male religious symbology sanctifies these distortions. As Mary Daly (1973) points out, "When God is a male, the male is God."

To speak of male dominance is also to speak of misogyny, hatred of women. Misogyny is manifested in the control of women by men, the erasure of women's history, the devaluation of women's work, the silencing of women's insight, the denial of women's experience, and the enduring violation of women that centuries of male rule bear witness to (Barry, 1979). From the burning of women on the stakes of Europe to foot-binding, from genital mutilation to Indian suttee, from the battering of wives at home to the harassment of women at work, from the rape of women inside and outside marriage to the vicious objectification of women in pornography, from legal attempts to deny us our bodies to moral restraints to deny us our loves, misogyny goes on and on. Under male colonization, women are objects to be used in the interest of the fathers to support their work, to promote their interests, and even to think their thoughts. Patriarchal definitions prevail, putting forth meanings that shape the fabric of our lives, even the deepest crevices of our imagination. Human oppression, then, is rooted in the structured evil of male supremacy.

Secondly, let us examine how this structured misogyny has affected human sexuality. Although my listing is illustrative rather than exhaustive, I shall comment on only three evils resulting from our approach to sexuality.

1. *Compulsory heterosexuality:*[1] The establishment of the heterosexual norm and the naming as deviant of any variation from that norm has exerted, as you know,

stringent controls on sexual expression. This practice has, in effect, contributed to male control of women and a valuing of woman only in so far as she is attached to a man. Recall the derogatory naming of women who are not so attached; e.g., old maid, spinster. From her earliest years, the girl child is socialized by numerous mechanisms to be wife and mother, and/or to assume work roles that duplicate her nurturing role in the family. Few, if any, other messages are given her. She learns that being a woman implies the assumption of particular values and behavior that are subordinate and heterosexual in nature.

The boy child is similarly socialized. He learns that being a man is equivalent to certain expected social responses. He comes to accept uncritically that women exist for his pleasure and that his work, his power, and his experience are primary. While these foundations are changing somewhat, we cannot deny that they still prevail as the predominant orientation of socialization (Bianchi & Ruether, 1976). It is essential to understand that enforced heterosexuality is a critical structural component of existing power arrangements.

Feminist theology invites a reconsideration of these norms. Feminists believe that love does not depend on gender and that the primacy of heterosexuality prevents women and men alike from exploring in a healthy way all the avenues of sexual expression. Such a limitation diminishes our capacity to fully image the breadth and depth of God and the marvelous range of sexuality open to human beings.

2. *Genital fixation:* I noted earlier the mind-body split that is inherent to patriarchal beings. The identification

of the male with disembodied mind produces the emotionless man, disconnected from his feelings, unable to communicate genuine sorrow, joy, or wonder. We are all familiar with the stereotype, "boys don't cry." The serious implications of this dualism include an inability to relate on the basis of feeling, a weakened capacity for intimacy, and a lessened appreciation for gestures of human caring, such as the beauty of caressing, holding and resting. These give way to efficient genital sex and a rush to orgasm.

With respect to religion, notions of genital fixation place the orgasmic act in a heightened privileged position and view it, not just as one expression of sexuality, but as a pristine moment to be shared only with a permanent partner. Such a perception, I believe, fails to take into account the diverse means of growth open to human beings. Feminist theological reflection affirms varied manifestations of human loving. Within the feminist order, there is no hierarchy of touch, only a steady consecration to deepened intimacy. For each of us such blessed intimacy is achieved in our own way and in our own time. Intuition, integrity, and faithful respect for self and the other provide guidance.

3. *Denial of the body:* I want to draw out further the consequences of the mind-body dualism for it seems to me that the failure to affirm embodiment is fundamental to the severe social problems we face (Nelson, 1978). I remind you that a denial of the body is a denial of women. To be embodied is to claim a posture of right relation, of connectedness. It is to experience oneself as a member of that vast commonwealth of being that in-

cludes all life, transcending both time and space. Disembodiment, on the other hand, fragments the tapestry of being and generates categories of otherness, of the objectification of persons different from ourselves, of the rejection of older persons and physically impaired persons as expendable and asexual; disconnection leads to disregard of the earth, pollution of the environment, national egoism and generational shortsightedness.

Theology from a feminist perspective gives centrality to our bodies/ourselves.[2] From this commitment an ethic of right relation emerges. In the sphere of technology, for example, feminist theology affirms measures which are safe, flexible, conserving of the environment and protective of the future. Feminist spirituality is one of right relation, biblical righteousness, a politic that experiences and is faithful to the organic concert of all being.

In summary, enforced heterosexuality, genital fixation and a denial of the body are elements of an ethic of dominance spawned by abusive male power and misogyny. Having discussed the roots of destruction and its effects on human sexuality, we now ask, "What is the particular contribution that lesbians and gay men can offer to generate the elimination of these conditions?" Here, I speak as a lesbian, as one who came to my identity and self affirmation through a winding and perilous route. I trace the geography of the lesbian journey in my own inner landscape as a passage of struggle and joy, and the never-ending summons to integrity. These transforming experiences solidify my bonds with my sisters and brothers in the lesbian and gay community. They also form the concrete basis of the following reflections.

It seems to me that the hard work of achieving and embracing a lesbian or gay male identity necessarily includes a confrontation with evil. Working through those forces which oppose us, we can see the myriad facets of social sin at their deepest levels and comprehend quite clearly the ways in which people are violated and victimized. This confrontation holds out the possibility of engendering in each one of us a profound determination for justice for ourselves and others. I suggest that the strength of our thirst for justice parallels the wholeness of our lesbian or gay male identity.

The work of unmasking the evil in sexual repression and of picking up that burden with the vision and vulnerability of our own lives, is a vivid act of faith. Announcing a new order of responsible sexual relatedness by embodying fresh dimensions of human freedom locates each of us on the spectrum of ongoing revelation and unfolding tradition. Our faithfulness to who we are shatters the foundations of outmoded social and religious beliefs and contributes to a veritable revolution in thought and feeling. Our presence is a radical upheaval of power arrangements by bodying forth relations of mutuality that are, I believe, the very life of God (Heyward, 1982).

In a real sense, then, our lives promote a new theology that fully integrates the beauty and diversity of sexual expression. How far this is from the body-denying patriarchal religious thought! Ours is a prophetic presence holding out promises of deepened humanization. Our lives are an invitation to others to reflect on their sexuality and their God, as well as a summons to explore the full meaning of embodiment. Only through the grace of generous love can we accomplish our vocation.

Finally, I want to conclude this chapter with notes on feminism for the wider struggle that engages us in an historical shift to overcome the ethics and practice of male dominance by the holy politics of feminism.

Feminism is essentially about conversion—the conversion of women from docility, passivity and silence to responsibility, freedom and speech and the conversion of men from aggression, competition and might to compassion, cooperation and care. Feminism is a politic that connects us with each other and roots us in the earth (Griffin, 1978). In this hour, it is a clarion call to repentance and a summons to forsake each and every barrier that diminishes the coming of justice and prevents the growth of love. Nothing can be the same, not in theology or ethics, not social customs or cultural institutions, not who we are ourselves or who we are to each other. Feminism puts a question mark beside everything and shakes every foundation. Nothing will remain the same.

Let us believe and be convinced that this is the work of our God renewing the earth, breathing the power of liberation into trembling hearts and minds, calling us to build an inclusive global community of love and justice and promising us the sustenance of life's power.

We cannot delay. Today, in this hour, let us put justice as a band upon our waist and faithfulness as a belt upon our hips. Let us renew the ancient covenant, build up the ancient ruins and restore the ruined cities. For the Spirit of God is indeed upon us all and we are annointed to live peace, to embody justice in our suffering and wounded world.

Notes

1. I have borrowed the term "compulsory heterosexuality" from the lesbian feminist poet, Adrienne Rich. See her article, "Compulsory Heterosexuality and Lesbian Experience." *Signs,* Spring, 1980.

2. Feminist ethicist Beverly Harrison, Union Theological Seminary, New York, gives primary emphasis to the lived world experience of women as a starting place for ethics. Watch for her forthcoming book.

References

Barry, K. *Female sexual slavery.* New Jersey: Prentice-Hall, 1979.

Bianchi, E., & Ruether, R. *From machismo to mutuality.* New York: Paulist Press, 1976.

Daly, M. *Beyond god the father.* Boston: Beacon Press, 1973.

Griffin, S. *Woman and nature.* New York: Harper & Row, 1978.

Heyward, C. *Toward the redemption of god: Toward a theology of mutual relation.* University Press, 1982.

Lifton, R. *The broken connection.* New York: Simon & Schuster, 1979.

Miller, J. B. *Toward a new psychology of women.* Boston: Beacon Press, 1976.

Nelson, J. *Embodiment.* Minneapolis: Augsburg Press, 1978.

Ruether, R. *New woman, new earth.* New York: Seabury Press, 1975.

PART TWO

Ecclesial Perspectives

Chapter Five

HOMOSEXUALITY, CELIBACY, RELIGIOUS LIFE AND ORDINATION

Robert Nugent

I SUSPECT that it comes as no surprise to read that the Roman Catholic Church has historically always numbered among its ordained clergy and vowed religious women and men individuals of a homosexual orientation. The Yale historian, Dr. John Boswell, in his massive and scholarly work, *Christianity, Social Tolerance and Homosexuality,* recently documented the existence of homosexual monastic and secular clerics in the middle ages (Boswell, 1980). He also described a kind of gay subculture which flourished in the 12th century monastic tradition. The intense same-sex and presumably celibate friendships in letters and poetry would result today only in having seminarians and novices expelled from theology schools and novitiates. If there is ever to be a canonized gay patron saint, Aelred of Rievaulx is everyone's favorite candidate.

Boswell noted two erotic verse letters from one religious woman to another found in a 12th century manuscript and characterized one letter as the outstanding example of medieval lesbian literature. Although Boswell's research covers only one period of church history, in-depth studies of other periods would certainly reveal similar findings. The extent and visibility of the phenomenon of gay and lesbian clergy and religious, however, would vary depending on political, social and ecclesiastical climates of the times.

If we accept Carl Jung's description of the homosexual personality, we could argue rather convincingly that there are many valid and honorable reasons to account for what many people suspect is a higher percentage of homosexual people in religious and church vocations than in the general population. According to Jung, homosexual people possess a particular receptivity to spiritual realities, a richness in religious feelings, a sensitivity to past values, and a conservative temperament in the best sense of that term (Jung, 1959). Other commentators have noted that lesbian and gay people seem drawn to nurturing professions such as teaching, nursing, and ministry and that many show a real concern for future generations in ways other than biological reproduction. At the present time we have no hard data on the percentage of gay and lesbian clergy and religious. Estimates, varying from 5 to 30 percent, from people in gay ministry can be termed only educated guesses.

If the presence of homosexual people in the clergy does not surprise people today, the increasing openness and publicity surrounding the issue do. No doubt some coverage is marred by sensationalism, curiosity and faddism. Manipulation by and of the press, individual immaturity, and institutional intimidation and fear have also contributed to inaccurate and distorted impressions. Nevertheless, there are examples of some honest and responsible exposure of this very sensitive aspect of church life which has helped raise the issue considerably in the general consciousness of the church. A recent case is the six-part series on gay Catholic and Protestant clergy that appeared in the summer of 1981 in a Milwaukee paper (Patrinos, Legro, Bednarek and Fauber, 1981). The months and weeks preceding publication, however, were filled with threats, rumors, anxiety and not a little paranoia on all sides.

The issue of homosexual clergy and religious is very much a taboo topic, especially with the added pressure of the slightest ambiguity about the genuineness of a celibate commitment in theory or practice. Yet the topic refuses to go away. Two recent popular Catholic novels (Greeley, 1981; Kennedy, 1981) both include homosexual priests in the cast of characters. In the past two years, two publicly identified gay priests have been disciplined by Church authorities for actions stemming from public involvement in the issue of homosexuality (Turner, 1981; Overman, 1981). Several years ago the Roman Sacred Congregation for Religious attempted to prevent a retreat for gay women religious in this country (Winiarski, 1979). Another retreat program for men, however, went either unnoticed or raised less anxiety than the one for women. In the *National Catholic Reporter,* Washington Bureau Chief Arthur Jones (1981) warned his readers, "Do not discount the possibility of a major scandal. The percentage of homosexual seminarians and priests increases; the pattern of the times is that homosexuals are more likely to be active than passive (p. 28)."

In this chapter concerning homosexuality, celibacy,

religious life and ordination, I would first like to present an historical overview of recent church documents dealing with gay candidates for priesthood and religious life. Secondly, I will briefly address the topic of celibacy. Thirdly, I will discuss the problematic issues of admission policies and formation programs as they relate to homosexuality. Lastly, this chapter will examine some directions for the 80s in which the church must move freely and faithfully in facing homosexuality, ordination and religious life.

Historical Overview of Church Documents

In 1961 the Sacred Congregation for Religious circulated a letter dealing with the examination of male candidates for priesthood and religious life. It says in part:

> If a student in a minor seminary has sinned gravely against the sixth commandment with a person of the same or opposite sex or has been the occasion of grave scandal in the matter of chastity, he is to be dismissed as stipulated in Canon 1371 (Harvey, 1971, p. 45).

An exemption is to be made in the case of a "boy who has been seduced and who is gifted with excellent qualities and is truly penitent or when the serious sin was an objectively imperfect act (p. 45)." The same document also stipulates that a novice or professed religious who has not made perpetual vows should be treated more severely in the same sort of sin against chastity by being either dismissed or sent away, presumably to another location. A perpetually professed religious should be excluded from any further order, and deacons are to be reduced to the lay state. The letter also insists that clerics or religious who have sinned gravely against chastity with another person not be admitted even on a trial basis to the priesthood or to perpetual vows unless there is clear evidence of excusing causes or circumstances which can at least diminish responsibility in conscience. According to one commentator, this exception has traditionally been applied rather generously. However, when speaking of homosexual orientation the letter allows no exception: "Advancement to religious vows and ordination should be barred to those who are inflicted with evil tendencies to homosexuality or pederasty for whom the common life and the priestly ministry would constitute serious dangers (p. 46)." The letter also links homosexuality with neurotic symptoms and suggests that such a person would need a continual act of heroism to remain celibate and would most probably be chronically unhappy.

In the early 70s the United States Bishops' Committee on Pastoral Research and Practices (1973), chaired at that time by Archbishop James Hickey, published a document entitled "Principles to Guide Confessors in Questions of Homosexuality." This is the most detailed exposition of traditional theological and pastoral ministries to homosexual people to date from any official U. S. source, although the general letters from Archbishop John Quinn and Archbishop Rembert Weakland have been more recent.

In this document, under a section called "The Seminarian, Religious and Priest," a distinction is made between "passing homosexual proclivities" and "a real homosexual orientation." Psychiatric help is advised for the latter because in the author's view "generally speaking, the person has other problems besides the homosexual orientation (p. 12)." Admitting of complex situations which depend on the individual involved, the document suggests that the central question is "whether the person will have such great difficulties in the practice of complete chastity that he will be constantly unhappy (p. 13)." Doubts are to be resolved in favor of the church because dismissal of the individual will avoid subsequent spiritual and emotional harm to the person and scandal to the church.

In the case of those in final vows or ordained, the document again distinguishes between those who for a variety of reasons occasionally engage in homosexual behavior and those who are so deeply steeped in the homosexual way of life that they are convinced that it is either not sinful or, at least, not sinful for them. The author calls these "verbal rationalizations" and suggests that the individuals should be helped by both spiritual and psychological means to complete rehabilitation because "they really want to be chaste (p. 13)." One such model of this ministry is a program for male religious and clerics called "Rest, Renewal and Recreation" (Harvey, 1979).

The 1980 draft of the New Code of Canon Law says nothing specific about homosexual candidates for priesthood and religious life. Canon 212 simply says that only those young men would be admitted to the seminary who are judged capable of dedicating themselves perpetually to the sacred ministry. The same canon, however, makes mention of the psychological and physical health of the candidates and their human, social, spiritual and intellectual qualities. Under the rubric "psychological health," it is certainly possible that some individuals might find reasons for barring some, if not all, homosexually oriented candidates for ordination or vows. This seems to be the position of the committee of the bishops of New England in their policy paper on vocations, about which I will comment later.

The new "Plan for Priestly Formation," does not deal directly with the issue of homosexuality or homosexual candidates (NCCB Committee on Priestly Formation, 1980). In fact, the Plan seems to indicate that there will be no homosexual candidates. It speaks of the seminarian as having "a sensitive appreciation of women and natural attraction to them (p. 23)." The document does state that college seminarians must "have made serious progress in finding their identity in sex (p. 117)" and urges "education in the realities of human sexuality (p. 21)" including homosexuality.

Celibacy

Keeping in mind the above overview of church documents dealing with gay candidates for priesthood and religious life, I now turn to some remarks regarding celibacy. I wish to state from the very outset that when I use words like "homosexual," "lesbian," or "gay" in reference to clergy and religious, I am referring solely to sexual *orientation* and not to sexual behavior, unless otherwise noted. It is crucial to keep this fundamental distinction in mind. It is my experience that its neglect or misunderstanding has been a prime source of much tension and conflict on the part of many intelligent and generally sensitive church ministers and authorities. Too often the phrase "homosexual orientation" automatically implies sexual activity and we incorrectly assume that a homosexual orientation is always accompanied by sexual behavior.

As a church, we say that homosexual celibates are a possibility. In fact, we hold out a life of complete sexual abstinence as the only proper pastoral approach. At the same time, we are uncomfortable whenever gay and lesbian celibates publicly identify themselves as such, or when self-acknowledged homosexual people who feel personally called to celibacy present themselves to our seminaries and religious communities for admission. In some official quarters there even seems to be a certain distrust of the gay celibate (Nugent, 1979). In a document that originated in the Sacred Congregation for Religious (1979) regarding a proposed retreat for gay women religious the author stated that support of justice for homosexual people runs the risk of appearing to support homosexual activity especially "in those instances when the priest or religious 'comes out' or openly declares himself or herself to be 'gay' or homosexual, even when such a declaration is accompanied by a slogan such as 'gay and celibate' (p. 2)."

It is not my place here to discuss the feasibility or desirability of the church's continuing to link celibacy with ordained ministry, although I certainly believe the issue is a crucial one in the life of the church. As Schillebeeckx (1981) writes in *Ministry,* there are some unanswered questions about the anthropologically inner relationship between sexuality and love. Present church legislation on celibacy seems to leave this question unanswered and thus poses the following dilemma: does physical abstinence of itself ever have a religious value (hard to affirm if we do not want to promote an anti-sexuality attitude)? Or is it a matter of degree of competition between love for God and love for a fellow human being? In response to the objection that a completely chaste life was necessary for the highest mystical experience, Thomas Merton is reported to have said that "conditions had changed and that celibacy even for a monk was a thing of the past (Rice, 1970, p. 135)."

Given the teaching of the church on human sexuality and Christian marriage, it would be naive to think that any change in the area of celibacy would have any effect on gay clergy and religious. The issue today for both homosexual and heterosexual clergy and religious is that of mature, loving relationships with both sexes. Such relationships reflect God's love, support us in our ministry, help us cope with the human experience of loneliness, and witness to the values of a free commitment to celibacy for the kingdom.

Psychological research indicates that the incidence of sexual difficulties and immaturities is no greater nor less among celibates than among non-celibates. Despite this fact, there have been for far too long the experience and impression of cold, frightened and insensitive celibates whose human growth seems to have been stunted by an inauthentic kind of celibate lifestyle. Among males certainly this is due in some part to an inordinate and continually reinforced fear of close, same-sex friendships with the ever present suspicion of homosexuality hanging overhead. Fortunately, a more positive appreciation of chastity, the acknowledgment of the need for authentic intimacy, and congregational policies of accepting older candidates who have had some opportunity for sexual maturation have all contributed to a feeling that tomorrow's celibates will be effective signs of God's love and action in our human community.

We can and do separate sexual orientation from sexual behavior for purposes of teaching, discussion and de-emotionalizing the issue. By this distinction we can risk the danger of separating them so totally that they have almost no relationship to each other whatsoever. This approach does an injustice both to the concept and dynamics of human sexuality and to the people who identify themselves as homosexually oriented. A recent church document confirms this impression. In "Education for Human Sexuality for Christians," the United States Catholic Conference's Department of Education (1981) notes that "the person who is ostracized in his/her own Church community because of a homosexual orientation finds little comfort that the Church distinguishes between homosexual orientation and homosexual activity (p. 30)."

Refining and appreciating the connection between orientation and behavior will help us not only in working with those celibate individuals whose sexuality is expressed in acceptable but new and unfamiliar non-genital ways, but also in helping us to interpret and respond to sexual acting out among celibates. About this latter we can be neither naive nor unrealistic in light of a recent study which indicated that of some 50 diocesan and religious priests who identified themselves as homosexual, only two saw themselves as "celibate" in the church's traditional understanding of that term (Wagner, 1980).

In some instances church authorities have no choice but to make administrative decisions that are, it is to be hoped, just and compassionate in the case of individuals whose public behavior and lifestyle are in obvious contradiction to what the church expects of a celibate commitment. It makes no sense to cry "oppression" in those situations; however, the manner in which the situation is handled might involve serious violations of the most fundamental elements of due process. The expulsion of a priest from a diocese simply because he was seen in a gay club or the transfer of a sister to another assignment because she has been involved as a local Dignity chaplain is certainly not due process.

I am not referring to struggles to grow in a celibate commitment that are being handled maturely both individually and communally. Nor am I referring to those controversial personal conscience decisions about celibacy which some think necessary as part of an evolution in church life or as the first step in the implementation of the ancient doctrine of the *non receptio legis.* On the basis of this traditional teaching a valid church law can become irrelevant because it is no longer accepted in fact by the great majority of believers. To act on this principle, one must be willing to take the consequences in the same way as the nuclear weapons protestors expose themselves to arrest and imprisonment.

The situations to which I refer have a public impact upon a diocese or parish, a religious community or the larger Church. My remarks about homosexually active celibates apply equally to heterosexually active celibates. Unfortunately, however, I suspect that too often a subtle double standard exists when church leaders are responding to homosexual situations. We ought to be as deeply concerned about obvious violations of poverty and simplicity of life style and about the abuse of power in the church that can cause as much, if not more, "scandal" than violations of a celibate commitment.

Problematic Issues in Contemporary Church Life

Having referred to recent church documents and some remarks on celibacy as a context for this chapter, I will now discuss a third area which involves two problematic issues in contemporary church life directly affected by the topic of homosexuality: (1) admission policies and (2) formation programs.

(1) *Admission Policies:* Several years ago some bishops took part in a national meeting on vocations and religious formation among diocesan seminaries and male religious communities. Discussion among the participants surfaced a rather strong sense of discomfort with the quality of applicants to seminaries and religious communities. Bishop Ward of Los Angeles was quoted in the *National Catholic Reporter* as stating that "The he-man types don't seem to be interested in the seminary." He also expressed concern about the increase of "soft, if not effeminate seminarians" (Bourgoin, 1979, p. 17). One suggestion he offered was the return to a strong program of physical education in seminaries which might reduce the effeminacy.

In a similar vein but in another context, Archbishop Joseph Bernardin (1978), the new Archbishop of Chicago, told the American Bishops that "we're getting weaker candidates for the priesthood." While the word "weaker" bears a number of different interpretations ranging from physical to intellectual liabilities, the word in this context in certain church circles is often a code word for homosexual. One might recall Paul's description of God's using the "weak and powerless" things of the world to confound the "strong and wise."

In June, 1981, Bishop Walter Sullivan (1981) of Richmond, in a talk to Serra International disagreed with this analysis and judgment of "weak candidates."

> I would dispute those who claim that the priesthood today is attracting weaker candidates. Some qualities such as rugged individualism and impersonalism were seen in the past as attributes, but are now viewed as liabilities. Seminarians today are not softer or less manly because they strive to become warm and loving persons. With a better understanding and more frequent use of the behavioral sciences, seminarians, faculty members and vocation directors are discussing areas of concern heretofore never mentioned (p. 212).

In any case, there are indications that increasing numbers of self-acknowledged homosexual males are seeking admission to seminaries and religious orders. A parallel situation does not seem to exist among women's groups. This development has raised the issue of admission and formation policies of seminaries and communities regarding self-acknowledged homosexual applicants. Should a diocese or order have spelled out, at least to themselves, a clear policy on admission and formation principles for gay men and lesbian women who are honest and open about their sexual identity? I am not speaking of those candidates who are repressed, confused or pretending. These are important, to be sure, but are other problem areas. If there is to be a policy, who is involved in making it? On what grounds is the policy made; e.g., church laws, customs, the gospel, social studies, past experiences? How is the policy publicized and implemented?

There are some sound arguments against making any specific policy for a particular group. ("We like to treat all applicants alike.") But without a policy or at least a community study of the issue, it is quite possible that a particular applicant could be summarily rejected or accepted simply on the particular biases of a vocation director, seminary rector or formation personnel. It is especially likely that an openly gay or lesbian applicant will experience problems if there has been a past history of unpleasant or disruptive episodes involving homosexual candidates in a particular diocese or religious group.

Vocation directors, formation personnel and others need a good deal of basic education in the whole area of homosexuality if they are to be fair in their dealings with homosexual candidates. This includes the necessity of facing their own beliefs, feelings and experiences of homosexuality, gender identity and intimacy in relationships. These topics are still taboo in many communities and seminaries; as a result everyone suffers. For instance, there is a strong reluctance even to initiate open discussion among members of admission or formation teams about an applicant's homosexual orientation. Sometimes the fear stems from a desire *not* to appear judgmental or to discriminate against an individual when in reality the discussion might lead to the inevitable conclusion that this particular person ought *not* be admitted.

One common error is the confusion of sexual "orientation" with "gender role" or "gender appropriate behavior." This confusion is also involved in dealing with transsexuals or transvestites. It results in labeling males who exhibit certain characteristics, traits or interests categorized as "female" in our culture, as homosexual. It labels as "lesbian" women who exhibit socially approved "male" qualities, dress, interests or behaviors. In what is otherwise a generally good document on vocations and priestly formation, a Committee of the Bishops of New England (1980) declares categorically that "Young men who are excessively effeminate should not be admitted (p. 472)" to seminaries. While one could argue about the precise meaning of "excessively," there does seem to be a general agreement that the limp-wristed homosexual stereotype does not command respect as a priest and should not be admitted. At least this was the conclusion of the participants in the national vocation meeting I referred to above.

In 1979, a Sister of Charity attempted to ascertain congregational policies regarding lesbian and gay applicants (Sweeney, 1980). Her study was conducted with the 268 male and female communities serving the metropolitan New York area. Of the communities contacted, 175 were women's groups; 93, men's groups. The response rate of both the women's and men's groups was 25 percent; 43 women's groups and 26 men's groups responded. Only 1 out of 10 diocesan seminaries or seminary residences replied to the questionnaire. The results indicated that 11 communities have established policies of accepting homosexual candidates, 31 groups made individual assessments, 7 had a policy of not accepting homosexual candidates, and 20 responded that they were studying or about to study the issue. Two quotes will suffice to indicate the wide diversity of the responses:

> We would admit any woman who meets our qualifications including a healthy motivation, as far as we can assess, to live a celibate life. Homosexual orientation would not be a deterrent. The individualized formative guidance of the person who discloses a homosexual orientation would include discussions of celibacy and intimacy. Our Formation Committee hopes to work on this topic in more detail in the future (p. 8).

> We would not accept a celibate homosexual into our community primarily because we feel that this situation would present a constant source of difficulty, temptation and tension for the candidate in question. Religious life is demanding enough without any extra burdens . . . I think we should all be concerned with the very sad plight of a homosexual. We should do all we can to help a person so afflicted. But I think one of the most important ways in which to help the homosexual of our day is to bring him as close as possible to the Divine Physician, to the One Who truly understands the problem, Who has the only key to the solution of this problem. We must acknowledge homosexuality for what it really is—an aberration—and when freely indulged in, a serious sin before God (p. 26).

Obviously this is only a small sampling, although the response rate was encouraging. As a pilot study it provides some relevant data for discussion and future research. A similar study was reported by a Holy Cross priest of vocation directors of diocesan programs and religious communities, but the percentage of replies was even smaller (Oddo, 1978).

A homosexual orientation, apart from any homosexual behavior, is cause for serious and constant concern on the part of religious authorities. The Committee of New England Bishops (1980) again provides a striking example of this kind of thinking: "Young men who are truly homosexuals should not be admitted. We recognize that there are various degrees of homosexuality and that generalizations cannot easily be made. We include in this statement anyone who, while not engaging in homosexual activity, is psychically homosexual and thereby unable to tolerate the demands of a celibate priestly ministry or rectory living (p. 472)." (I know quite a number of healthy heterosexual clergy who cannot tolerate the demands of rectory living!) "So a man who seems unable to come to heterosexual maturity," continues the committee, "should not be admitted (p. 472)." This kind of attitude demands for ordination not only maleness but something which not even Jesus required: heterosexual celibacy.

This same attitude surfaces in a 1978 study of 12 male religious communities, "Trends in Seminary Formation," conducted by the Center for Applied Research in the Apostolate (Henderson, 1978). Through counseling and staff interviews with college seminarians, clinical evidence raises the question of "whether or not the personality qualities of at least some homosexuals do not indeed militate against success in religious communities (p. 12)." Many of those seen in counseling were hypersensitive, critical, jealous, demanding and possessive of friends. In the same report the author speaks of a workshop in California in 1978 where the consensus of the participants, who were directors of novices and other religious formation staff, was that "homosexuals should not be accepted for religious life (p. 12)."

The traditional attitudes and negative judgments about homosexuality in society, most religious groups and the legal and medical professions foster a non-accepting and even hostile environment for homosexually oriented persons. Consequently, there is serious reason for concern that gay and lesbian candidates might need assistance in handling any repressed anger, poor self-image, low self-esteem or other difficulties in such an environment. But we ought to give equal worth to a comment of the Catholic Social Welfare Commission (1981) of the Bishops of England and Wales. In speaking of the wide diversity of homosexual people the Commission includes "those who are well adjusted, stable people who have come to terms with their homosexuality, who never seek help and who are never in trouble with the law. These people are psychologically adjusted, sometimes even better than the average heterosexual (pp. 12–13)." This is even truer today when the impact of the gay liberation movement and the stress on self-acceptance and a positive self-identity have had some visible effect on young gay and lesbian people.

Naturally, every religious community and diocese is very much concerned about its public image, especially in terms of attracting new members. This is an old version of "What will the neighbors think?" Communities and dioceses are most unwilling to get a high profile either for gay ministry or for being particularly accepting of homosexual applicants. Most are moving to identification with the poor and oppressed in Latin America, but not with the lesbian and gay people in the United States. Fears and tensions arise when a community moves to educate itself on the issue of homosexuality.

These fears often paralyze efforts to raise the issue in other quarters. The stigma of guilt by association is still a powerful one. We hesitate to bring the topic of homosexuality to the attention of the larger group in newsletters, resource listing, chapter reports and other internal media for fear of arousing anxieties and even open opposition. Consequently, we neglect to provide sound and balanced information to help sensitize people to their gay and lesbian colleagues with whom they live and minister.

There are some bright spots on the horizon. There have been a number of workshops, lectures, study days, special committees, task forces and pastoral letters coming from communities and dioceses. Two striking examples include a pastoral letter by Archbishop Weakland (1980) entitled *Who Is My Neighbor?* and a "Dear Confrere" letter from Fr. Dismas Bonner, OFM (1981) provincial of the Chicago-St. Louis Sacred Heart Franciscans. The latter is a model of balance, sensitivity, pastoral challenge and courage which deserves wide circulation among religious communities.

"Is there a limit," Fr. Malloy (1981) asks "to the percentage of homosexuals that a given community can absorb without affecting the nature and quality of their life together?" He answers tentatively "it seems likely that a group with a fairly high percentage of homosexuals will take on some of the characteristics of the homosexual subculture (p. 352)," but his enumeration of those "characteristics" can be challenged as too stereotypical. He also mentions a possible danger that the heterosexual celibates in that community might be tempted to overcompensate by showing an intense concern for the "macho" or culturally approved ways of reinforcing one's masculine identity.

(2) *Formation Programs:* Apart from the ongoing task of integrating one's sexuality into a mature, celibate commitment, there are a number of related questions that seem pertinent to the formation programs for homosexual candidates. Once the individual has been accepted, the question inevitably arises concerning how free is she or he to share that identity with others such as peers or older members of the group, students, seminary staff or formation teams, bishops or provincials. I am not referring to a public announcement in the *New York Times* or even a tasteful interview in the *National Catholic Reporter*. But a simple and natural disclosure of one's human identity and existence, when and if appropriate, should be possible without undue fear or anxiety of rejection, anger, withdrawal, expulsion, gossip or false assumptions.

Most homosexual people in religious life and ministry today must cope with the tensions of not feeling free to share their sexual identity. Consequently, they are forced to live emotionally and psychologically double lives. The ideal situation is to create an atmosphere of trust in which a person will neither feel forced to deny nor compelled to disclose his or her sexual orientation. More and more gay and lesbian priests and religious are feeling an inner need either to identify publicly with the struggles of homosexual people in church and society or to come out to avoid a sense of personal hypocrisy or duplicity. The decision demands a great sense of discernment both for the individual and the group and ought not be made lightly or under pressures. It is not sufficient nor helpful to rail "One's sexual orientation is not really all that important, so why bother about it?" The question of public identification as lesbian or gay for a priest or religious involves the added pressure of a group celibate image. While that important reality should be part of the decision, I do not agree with Malloy (1981) when he writes, "At this moment in Church history the political and social meaning of such attestations is too ambiguous to be acceptable (p. 346)."

In the area of formation, communities do have certain expectations of gay and lesbian candidates. But the other side of the coin cannot be overlooked: gay and lesbian people also have a right to certain expectations that their own emotional health and growth will be respected and fostered on all levels. Some communities and dioceses ought *not* to accept openly gay and lesbian candidates but not because of any deficiency on the part of the candidates. Rather, some communities or dioceses cannot foster the personal or group integration of the homosexual individual without much tension, turmoil and harm both to the person and the group.

What is to be done for gay and lesbian priests and religious to ameliorate the quiet isolation they experience is difficult to ascertain. Very few groups have begun to address this issue even within the relative privacy of their own communities. Others have attempted responses that in some cases are helpful and constructive and in others crippling and destructive.

Spiritual directors today are facing new challenges in directing and counseling gay and lesbian people in formation programs. Some believe it better for gay and lesbian spiritual directors to direct homosexual people since they could more easily identify with the problems and struggles being faced and dealt with. Others suggest that such a situation might pose a real danger of false empathy or a tendency to avoid real challenges to growth in the directee.

Community retreats and workshops are also an area of concern because the real life situations of homosexual people are rarely addressed, or even noted in presentations. Talks on celibacy, chastity and inter-personal intimacy are always couched in heterosexual language and examples that do not relate directly to the lived experience of homosexual clergy and religious. It is falsely assumed that the entire listening audience is heterosexually oriented. Some of the concerns are certainly the same; but there are particular differences that ought to be explored and addressed. Given the need for peer support among any particularized and alienated population, there are valid reasons for specialized retreats, workshops and days of reflection. Although any indication of a separatist mentality needs to be strongly avoided, there is a need for ongoing association with other gay and lesbian clergy and religious. It is also possible that a conflict can arise when too much time or psychic energy is devoted to the gay subculture within or without the religious community.

The discomfort that many people experience when one speaks of gay or lesbian groupings in religious communities is due in some part to a fear of cliques, divisions or even threats to one's primary commitment to ministry or community. These fears are real and must be faced head on. The dangers involved need not prevent the good that can result from support groups with mature leadership and ongoing supervision. If communities and diocesan structures were more open, trusting and comfortable with their homosexual members, the danger of attempting to meet all one's needs outside the community might be considerably reduced or entirely eliminated.

The basic need for acceptance, trust and support must be found somewhere. Communities here and there are making some concerted efforts to educate the larger membership on the topic of homosexuality in order to pave the way for those members who will share their sexuality with others in the group. One common source of pain for many lesbian and gay religious and clergy is the harsh and judgmental prejudice manifested by coarse "queer jokes" and remarks about "faggots" often heard in community rooms or rectory dining areas.

Support groups for priests and religious men and women which meet for discussion, prayer, reflection, and even challenge in an atmosphere that is trusting and non-threatening are already beginning to emerge in a number of men's communities and several dioceses. At least two informal communications networks exist in the U.S. and Canada. In some places they function with the approval of provincial authorities; others meet privately and are known only by word of mouth.

These support groups are not organized to lobby, protest, recruit or demonstrate, nor do they form sexual liaisons, a fear that is expressed by some. Rather, they allow for sharing, growth, accountability, healing and reconciliation. They provide a sense of belonging and acceptance which many have not found elsewhere. Within these groups individuals cope in terms of the Christian value system with some problematic elements of the gay subculture.

Support groups are beginning to receive public recognition and approval from respected individuals like Dr. Thomas Kane, the priest-psychotherapist who heads the House of Affirmation near Boston. At the 1981 meeting of the National Federation of Priests' Councils in Memphis, Fr. Kane (1982) urged "that the significant number of priests with a homosexual orientation join and be encouraged to join support groups of other homosexual priests. New structures need to be implemented for the pastoral support and care of the priest who is homosexual (p. 18)." Some of the programs already formulated to provide priestly renewal on a diocesan or communal basis, such as Fr. Vince Dwyer's Emmaus program, could easily incorporate specific support groupings for gay clergy and religious.

Directions for the 80s

In the preceding pages, I have reviewed some recent church documents concerning homosexuality, the priesthood and religious life, discussed celibacy and treated the two problematic issues of admission policies and formation programs. Finally, I would like to pose three directions for the 80s which the church must realistically face: (1) the relationship between a homosexual orientation and homosexual behavior, (2) ministry to our gay and lesbian ministers, and (3) a major study to gather data on the experiences of homosexual celibates.

(1) *Orientation—Behavior Relationship:* We need to articulate more clearly those fundamental judgments about a homosexual orientation in and of itself apart from any sexual or genital behavior. We must re-examine our personal and communal judgments about a homosexual orientation with as much data as we can ob-

tain from a variety of sources, especially the empirical sciences. The 1981 publication of the Kinsey Institute, *Sexual Preference: Its Development in Men and Women,* provides us with the most current information on the genesis of a homosexual orientation and offers a sound critique of some of the more popular beliefs about the part that parents play in that process (Bell, Weinberg & Hammersmith, 1981).

We base many of our attitudes, policies, decisions and practices on our own deeply rooted beliefs, fears, values and anxieties about sexuality, male and female identities and relationship, and homosexuality. Officially, church statements view homosexual orientation as neutral, not freely chosen and, consequently, not open to condemnation as such. (This position separates us from some of the more biblically literal denominations.) If this is so, then we should be able to progress in overcoming our fears about the topic and face it more calmly, honestly and realistically in ourselves and others. We should also be more comfortable in supporting those who claim this identity for themselves, provided they are not attempting to exhaust their whole self-definition simply in terms of sexual orientation. We can encourage them to explore its implications for their own lives and ours and even to share it publicly at appropriate times without fear of censure, hostility or isolation. Again, I am speaking here of orientation, not behavior. Our experience of sexuality has an effect on the way we pray, minister, relate to God and others, experience community and church. Gay and lesbian people must be given opportunities to articulate these experiences for the good of the whole community.

Part of coming to grips with sexual identity is communicating that reality to others either verbally or nonverbally. Making it somehow public, especially in those instances where it has an impact upon one's living and one's relationships with others, seems to contribute to one's self-acceptance and adjustment.

Because of our tendency to confuse orientation with behavior, the issue of "coming out" causes bishops and religious administrators to become nervous. They maintain that people are not ready for such revelations, ministry can be undermined, the credibility of a celibate commitment is at stake, vocations will suffer, people will be confused, hurt and scandalized, and parents will fear for the welfare of their children. The question of public disclosure of a celibate's homosexual orientation must be faced if we are to make any advance in ministry to gay and lesbian celibates in our religious families and dioceses.

On the other hand, if we believe that a homosexual orientation is somehow less good or desirable, less fully human or complete, a handicap or a form of arrested psychological development, a "result of the fall," morally neutral but not psychologically or socially neutral, then we will be hesitant to offer it to others. We will view it as a flaw in human development. The issue is not public vs. private disclosure, but one's underlying judgment about the orientation itself. Consistency demands that our fundamental judgments regarding the public ministry and open disclosure of gay or lesbian religious or priests and any limitations put on them must also be applied equally to other public ministries that are currently being developed in the community or "services" such as ministers of communion, readers, deacons, pastoral workers, and religious educators.

We will also need to give more serious study to the distinction between orientation and behavior. In particular, church people have concentrated entirely too much on behavior and have failed to develop sensitivities to other aspects of homosexuality and the impact it has on other areas of one's life. Andrew Greeley wrote recently about the positive effects on a man's spirituality when he images God as female, but he noted that such an approach would not appeal to gay and lesbian people and that more thought needs to be given to those situations.

(2) *Ministry to Ministers:* Provincials, bishops, spiritual directors and other religious administrators are becoming more and more aware of those clergy or religious who come to an awareness or acceptance of their homosexual orientation only later in life. This seems to happen with more frequency among women religious than among males, but the issues and the questions are similar. What are our responsibilities to these people? This traumatic time can precipitate other related crises such as vocation decisions, alcoholic or chemical dependency, intimacy issues, ability to relate and minister, sexual acting out and months or even years of confusion, anxiety and guilt.

Until very recently, the major ministerial outreach group to gay priests and religious has been the lay organization called Dignity. This group has provided space for clergy and religious to find at least some semblance of understanding, support and a non-judgmental atmosphere while they sort out many things in their lives. At times peer counseling, unconditional affirmation and a gradual shedding of defenses, pretenses, and shame have led to a healthier integration and a recommitment to celibacy and priesthood or religious life. Anyone who has had contact with the organization cannot help but notice the intense feeling of care and communal spirit that is expressed in and among people who have shared similar experiences of rejection and self-doubt. What gradually develops is a fine sense of self-worth and affirmation that is so crucial to individuals struggling with sexual orientation in the context of previous commitments to celibacy and religious vows.

No doubt today the most sensitive area causing most of the tension for church authorities is the question of sexual-genital expression among committed celibate members. Neither can we deny its existence nor should we panic and overreact. The principles, responsibilities and pastoral concerns that are operative in parallel situations with heterosexuals are the same. What we have to avoid is a tendency to allow a double standard to operate. We often seem more willing to view heterosexual behavior as a temporary and passing experience, a struggle to grow, dissatisfaction with work, authority conflicts, human weakness or loneliness. In similar cases with homosexual behavior there seems to be less patience in working with these possibilities and a tendency to settle the problem immediately with expulsion, transfer, suspension or other punishments designed to avoid scandal at all costs.

Some efforts have been made to provide guidance for religious superiors dealing with homosexual behavior among celibate members. In 1978, for instance, a group of seven Jesuit psychiatrists prepared recommendations which begin with the generally agreed-upon premise that overt homosexual activity is incompatible with faithful observance of a life of celibacy (Gill, 1980). In keeping with their psychoanalytic background they agreed that homosexual behavior itself is to be regarded as "sexually disordered and generally representing impaired personality development (p. 25)." This judgment is open to quite serious challenge from the psychiatric profession as evidenced from the 1973 reclassification by the American Psychiatric Association. "Because homosexual behavior in a religious person frequently manifests serious emotional disturbance," the Jesuit psychiatrists said, "it warrants a psychologic or psychiatric evaluation . . . and treatment (p. 25)." They agreed unanimously that "a religious person who is either unable or unwilling to resolve" the problem of repeated homosexual behavior "is unsuitable for life in an order or congregation that understands the vow of chastity or celibacy in the same way the Church does (p. 25)." They were careful to point out that they regarded externally expressed homosexual behavior no more morally objectionable than overt heterosexual activity if deliberately chosen by vowed celibates. We might question, however, whether they would recommend the heterosexual celibate for psychiatric evaluation and treatment.

In a church that prizes celibacy and an all-male clergy and rejects all homosexual behavior under any circumstances, it is somewhat curious to note that the very attempts to maintain an all-male clergy at any cost also promote in very subtle ways a strong homosocial climate as quite acceptable and ordinary. Does the introduction of a married clergy or women priests threaten in any way the male collaborative structure and the homosocial world of both heterosexual and homosexual clergy? But the homosexual issue cuts both ways. When the Episcopal Church was discussing the ordination of women, it was whispered rather loudly among certain clerical circles that the only women who really wanted to be ordained were lesbian. In our own Catholic community the Women's Ordination Conference has had to struggle with the issue of open support for gay and lesbian people at the risk of having the opponents of the ordination of women in the Roman Catholic Church hurl the same charge.

(3) *Future Study:* Finally, we would do well to undertake a major study on homosexuality involving bishops, theologians, pastoral workers, social scientists, biblical scholars and gay and lesbian Christians. We might even hope to build ecumenically on some of the studies of other Christian denominations. A thorough and solid study of the Catholic experience of the celibate lifestyle would provide an opportunity to support and enhance the authentic celibate commitments that already exist. It might also allay the suspicions that celibacy is neither desirable nor possible. It could just as well cause us to temper somewhat our claims about celibacy and help bridge the gap that seems to exist between the ideal and the lived reality. If we include in the study those lesbian and gay people who have freely and voluntarily attempted to live out the church's expectations, the data analysis will doubtless affect the pastoral advice we offer homosexual Christians about their responsibilities. I am not suggesting we arrive at moral decisions or policies by counting noses. But we cannot afford to ignore the experiences of those who live celibacy in a way that is integrating, humanly fulfilling, enriching and a blessing for the church community. Neither can we afford to ignore the experience of those who find it otherwise.

References

Bell, A., Weinberg, M. S., & Hammersmith, S. K. *Sexual preference: Its development in men and women*. Bloomington: Indiana University Press, 1981.

Bernadin, J. Other voices. *National Catholic Reporter*. December 12, 1978, 4.

Bonner, D. Letter to confreres. St. Louis, MO: Chicago-St. Louis Province of the Sacred Heart, August 5, 1981.

Boswell, J. *Christianity, social tolerance and homosexuality*. Chicago: University of Chicago Press, 1980.

Bourgoin, M. F. Tuesday afternoon with the bishops. *National Catholic Reporter,* January 19, 1979, 5, 17.

Catholic Social Welfare Commission. *An introduction to the pastoral care of homosexual people*. Mt. Rainier, MD: New Ways Ministry, 1981.

Committee of New England Bishops. Priestly formation: Discerning vocations. *Origins,* January 3, 1980, 9 (29), 467–476.

Committee on Pastoral Research and Practices. *Principles to guide confessors in questions of homosexuality*. Washington, D.C.: National Conference of Catholic Bishops, 1973.

Gill, J. Homosexuality today. *Human Development,* 1980, 1 (3), 16–25.

Greeley, A. *The cardinal sins*. New York: Warner Books, 1981.

Harvey, J. Homosexuality and vocations. *The American Ecclesiastical Review,* 1971, 164, 42–55.

Harvey, J. Reflections on a retreat for clerics with homosexual tendencies. *Linacre Quarterly,* May, 1979, 136–140.

Henderson, G. G. *Trends in seminary formation*. Washington, D.C.: CARA, 1978.

Jones, A. Play and stay priests. *National Catholic Reporter,* October 16, 1981, 28.

Jung, C. G. *The collected works,* trans. R. F. C. Hull. New York: Pantheon, 1959.

Kane, T. The priest: An affirmation of human sexuality. *The Priest,* 1982, 38, 13–18.

Kennedy, E. *Father's day*. Garden City, New York: Doubleday, 1981.

Malloy, E. *Homosexuality and the christian way of life.* Washington, D.C.: University of America Press, 1981.

National Conference of Catholic Bishops Committee on Priestly Formation. *Revised plan for priestly formation.* Washington, D.C.: NCCB/USCC, 1980.

Nugent, R. Silencing of gay issues in the christian churches. *Insight,* Summer, 1979, 7–9.

Oddo, T. Gays in priesthood and religious life. *Insight,* Summer, 1978, 2 (4), 5–7.

Overman, S. Miami archdiocese reassigns homosexual priest from parish to research. *National Catholic News Service,* December 3, 1981, 2.

Patrinos, D., Legro, R., Bednarek, J. and Fauber, J. Churches face major issues in the 80s. *Milwaukee Sentinel,* June 1–6, 1981.

Rice, E. *Man in the sycamore tree.* Garden City, New York: Doubleday, 1970, 135.

Sacred Congregation for Religious and Secular Institutes. *Observation on the proposed retreat for gay women religious.* Rome: Sacred Congregation for Religious and Secular Institutes, 1979.

Schillebeeckx, E. *Ministry.* New York: Crossroad, 1981.

Sullivan, W. The priesthood seminarians prepare for. *Origins,* September 17, 1981, 2 (14), 211–215.

Sweeney, W. *Congregational policies regarding lesbian/homosexual candidates.* New York: Intercommunity Center for Justice and Peace, 1980.

Turner, W. Outspoken homosexual priest warned. *New York Times,* February 27, 1981.

United States Catholic Conference. *Education in human sexuality for christians.* Washington, D.C.: USCC, 1981.

Wagner, R. *Gay Catholic priests: A study of cognitive and affective dissonance.* San Francisco: The Institute for Advanced Study of Human Sexuality, 1980.

Weakland, R. Who is my neighbor? *Milwaukee Catholic Herald,* July 19, 1980, 3.

Winiarski, M. Vatican ban on gay retreat sidestepped. *National Catholic Reporter,* May 18, 1979, 1, 5.

Chapter Six

CIVIL RIGHTS IN A CHURCH OF COMPASSION

Theresa Kane

SCRIPTURE is something that we read so often and yet can find to be ever new. In a recent reading of the gospel of Luke, I was struck very strongly and in a new way by the reading of Luke 17:20–36, which made me ask: "Am I lesbian?" It seems to me that homosexuality is part of us all.

In this specific passage Jesus is talking about his return and how we should act. When the Son of God returns again, he says, if you are on the rooftop, you should not go down and get your belongings which are in the house. Neither should the one in the field return home. Those who try to preserve their lives will lose them. Jesus also provides us an additional scenario about the last days. On that night, he says, there will be two men in one bed and one will be taken and the other left. Two women will be grinding grain together; one will be taken and the other left. Is it a stretch of the imagination to hold that in highlighting the relationship of a man to a man and a woman to a woman the scriptural writers have given us a clue to Jesus' own attitudes toward persons of homosexual orientation? I think not.

In this chapter I would like to share very briefly with you two experiences that introduced me to the whole question of homosexuality, especially concern for and with gay persons in the church. Secondly, I would like to offer some specific responses to Robert Nugent's chapter, "Homosexuality, Celibacy, Religious Life, and Ordination." Finally, I will articulate three challenges as we look at the issue of homosexuality in our church. My points, though certainly not meant to be exclusive, come from my own experiences and reflections.

Since early 1979, I and five members of the general administrative team of the Sisters of Mercy of the Union had two experiences that brought us into the middle of the homosexuality question. The first was our endorsement of the Catholic Coalition for Gay Civil Rights statement distributed by New Ways Ministry. The second was opening our generalate motherhouse, then located in Potomac, Maryland, to a workshop on homophobia in the churches sponsored by the Quixote Center. Those two actions, I believe, influenced our own understanding of the pain of lesbian and gay people in our church.

Regarding the gay rights statement we had diverse response from our own members. Some appreciated what we were doing and applauded us; others criticized us for shocking and scandalizing them. Our stand on gay rights reached a serious tension point during our chapter, notably over the question of civil rights for teachers. Let me parenthetically add that this consciousness-raising had the pleasant effect of convincing one of our province administrative teams to also endorse the Catholic Coalition for Gay Civil Rights statement.

The second action, the use of our facility for a homophobia workshop, immediately raised the question of how the local bishop would react. Since he was not in agreement with the Quixote Center's approach to homosexuality, would he attempt to control or stop the workshop or the use of our facility? We further observed that some of our sisters who lived and worked in the facility were so upset about our hosting this program that they left the generalate for the weekend. This taught us how our personal convictions can actually determine the kind of control we exert on physical facilities—facilities we say we do not own but hold in stewardship for the good of our community and of our church.

If the General Administrative Team of the Sisters of Mercy had said "No" to either request put to us, I probably would not be writing this chapter. The Sisters of Mercy would be headed in another direction. Within our community two strong reactions were hope and trust. Unfortunately, fear equally dominated. This concerns me greatly. At times this fear had been severe, extreme, irrational, even very violent. The question which this reaction has raised for me is: "How can professional religious who claim to be public Christians be so fearful?" What this says to me is that religion continually either frees or binds us with shackles. We are moving either into greater freedom or into greater bondage. Our response to homosexual persons indicates the direction we are taking.

Having shared these two significant events within my own religious community which helped to shape my thinking and attitudes on homosexuality, I wish to offer a few reflections on Robert Nugent's chapter, particularly in the light of my own experience. I believe, for women religious (I cannot speak for men religious) the issue of homosexuality has not yet surfaced publicly.

This is because we are very afraid to let it do so. On the whole, women religious do not know how to handle lesbianism. We do not seem able to garner the psychic energy and the creativity that a response demands. I can only conclude that I believe that we are homophobic, that we truly are afraid of homosexual persons. This presents a challenge to us as religious congregations. We need to free ourselves from our psychic fears and confront that issue, rather than to be afraid of it. I believe that the key is education. In this regard I have particularly appreciated the efforts of New Ways Ministry to dialogue with the bishops. We need to increase our dialogue with the bishops in this matter.

Nugent's chapter also raised for me the question of scandal. As a church we have emphasized personal moral scandal. We are becoming more conscious that we now have to give more attention and be equally concerned about the institutional scandal that is a part of our church.

Inner-church tensions are mounting because persons are afraid to look at the issue of homosexuality. This fear is generated from a strong conviction held by some concerning a precise identification of the issue and a necessary approach and from the threat of those who advocate a new thinking on homosexuality. Our tensions and conflicts will become more strained and intense as we move seriously into the issue.

I also wish to address a few remarks to the area of vows as presented in Nugent's chapter. There was a study conducted during the last few years by the Leadership Conference of Women Religious on issues of importance to religious congregations. A noteworthy omission was the vows, which says something about the direction we are taking as apostolic women religious. Within our own community, with the exception of formation personnel, we have not addressed the question of religious vows in any serious manner for about ten years. At the same time we have been looking very seriously at questions of service and ministry to our church and world. I cannot help but think that this may very well influence our future understanding of religious life.

My final reflection is taken from a feminist theologian. Having attended a conference of lesbian women, the theologian said it was the most exciting, most invigorating gathering she had witnessed in a long time. These women seemed so alive that she could not help but contrast them with the virgins of the third and fourth centuries who were very influential in setting church direction.

Having shared these few responses to "Homosexuality, Celibacy, Religious Life, and Ordination," I will now offer three serious challenges in regard to homosexuality. These challenges are for all of us in the church as we look at the question of lesbian and gay rights. First, as a church we need to be committed to what I call a stance of compassion, the human response to others characterized by the absence of a judgmental attitude. I do believe that this is important because we often know our church as judgmental. We need to be compassionate and truly in touch with one another as human beings, as people. We so quickly offer answers to questions before they are even raised. In this regard, it is very important for us to develop the feminist, intuitive side of the church. (Certainly the masculine side has already been developed.)

Jesus was intuitive. He was drawn to people because

he sensed their true worth, even though many were on the margins of society. The examples of his being with the outcasts are many. Jesus affirmed the dignity of every person and thereby crushed stereotypes. In his life he gave evidence that those who are lowly are to be raised up and the proud put down. That is a challenge to each of us and to the church since there are many 20th century outcasts. In any way people are lowly they need to be raised up to the fullest dignity that is theirs. I believe that in our contemporary church lesbian and gay persons are among the lowly to be exalted.

The proliferation of church regulations and directives creates a counter-response to true compassion. Because of these norms we have a real credibility gap as a church. The difference between what is official church prescription and what is our lived experience is further widening the gap. In this all of us are called to reshape the vision and the mission of the church. We need to do so courageously and compassionately while also trying to be as nonjudgmental as possible.

The second challenge regarding homosexuality in the church relates to sexism and sexuality. The feminist movement both influences and is influenced by the question of homosexuality. The feminist movement will continue to force our whole church to grapple with the question of sexuality, and relatedly with questions of heterosexuality and homosexuality. If we just look at church structures, it can be seen that one of the reasons the question is so crucial is that decisions on matters pertaining to human sexuality have been advanced without the participation of half of the church, the women. This has brought about not only a deficiency in our teaching, but a distortion. We cannot continue to deal with sexual issues in the church without the active inclusion of women.

Sexism is violence. Power in the church is related to that sin of sexism. Because we have violent expressions of sexism as a church, we also fail to advance the peace movement. We can not overlook this connection. We are called to be peacemakers, to be a strong part of the peace movement, but if we are going to continue to be violent in subtle or blatant ways we cannot truly look at the peace movement intrinsically.

A real call to counter sexism and to come to terms with sexuality involves a change in our way of imaging God. To continue to image God only as a male is a distortion of God as well as a distortion of our own sexuality. This very strong call is part of the challenge. And it is addressed to all of us. If we do not begin to image God in a new way, we are not going to address sexuality issues in a creative way.

The third challenge that I would pose involves the question of diversity and dissent. We need to foster diversity attitudinally and structurally as an enriching reality. We need to commit ourselves as a church to grow in as pluralistic a way as possible and to lessen expressions of uniformity. It has been stated that conflict is at the core of the Christian message, that Jesus was in conflict, that the message of Christianity is a conflictual one, and that conflict is needed if we are going to grow in an atmosphere of creative tension. Conflict involves suffering which we must embrace positively as a creative component of change. Dissent is essential for growth. It demands interior freedom, an informed, maturing conscience, and a conviction of action growing both from a courageous heart and an inspired mind. In looking at the challenge of diversity and dissent, we need a faith orientation, a faith stance. As Christians we act from what we believe.

Truly we are called to be on a journey. As we engage in that journey, each of us will be with God and God will be among us. We are called to continuous movement forward. Not to go ahead is to fall back. Conversion, therefore, is what is demanded of us. Part of the act of being transformed is to do what we can to reshape the face of our church. The task of conversion is what we are about.

Chapter Seven

GAY MEN AND WOMEN AND THE VOWED LIFE

Cornelius Hubbuch

ONE time a priest was preaching a retreat at a mental hospital. Concerned about focusing his listeners' obviously limited attention span on the meaning of life, he repeated continuously his theme: "Why are we all here?" He repeated it at the opening, the ending, and frequently in the course of each of his talks. On the second day, he was just ending once again with his question "Why are we all here?" when a frail little old lady who had been sitting quietly in a wheel chair, her lap covered with an afghan, piped up cheerily and with uncanny insight: "We're all here because we ain't all there."

I believe that this story says something about us as well as about the inmates of the institution: namely, we are not "all there" either, especially as we take a controversial step in our journey through life to seek the truth about personhood and human relationships.

In no way do I present, therefore, this response to Robert Nugent's sensitive and comprehensive chapter on "Homosexuality, Celibacy, Religious Life and Ordination" as an expert on the topic. I share with you some pastoral insights and opinions that have come to me as a member of a religious congregation of brothers for 28 years, as a teacher and high school principal for 16 years, and as a Provincial Superior of 183 men for the past six years.

Before exploring more specific issues, I wish to offer some of my opinions or assumptions as I approach the topic of human sexuality in general.

First Opinion: I believe the whole topic of homosexuality needs to be situated under the broader umbrella of human sexuality. The Catholic Church needs a deeper and more honest understanding based on our human experience and a clearer theology of what it means to be a person and what it means to be a sexual person.

For too long our Church has approached human sexuality in a negative way. We need to be more honest, realistic, and holistic in identifying life-giving ways of expressing our sexuality. If sexuality is at the very heart of the human person, then we need to be in touch with how to freely and responsibly express ourselves as sexual persons.

Second Opinion: The Church should develop and encourage theologizing from our lived experience. From our own personal experiences and from our pastoral experiences with others, we need to look for threads and patterns and then have theological reflection on that experience. Our Church in the United States is caught in the crosswinds of our traditional, medieval and Western philosophy and the theology of liberation now so much a part of the South American experience.

Third Opinion: The Church needs to develop and express a more comprehensive theology of personhood and of personal relationships. Do not our new understandings from psychology and the social sciences lead us to challenging questions about what is natural? According to Gregory Baum (1974):

> . . . the reason for this is not the influence of existentialism or what is sometimes called situation ethics—this represents too individualistic an emphasis to fit into the Catholic tradition—but rather, the realization, derived from the analysis of culture and society, that what is called human nature has a history and is, in part at least, created by people, their interaction and their symbolic language. Human nature is not simply a given. It is a given for the individual born into a specific environment, but looked upon historically and collectively, human nature has been created by the actions of people bound together by institutions and a common set of symbols (p. 480).

Given our new insights, therefore, what is sometimes called human nature could be, in fact, dehumanizing. An obvious current example would be to hold that men are superior to women. Quoting Baum again, "What is normative for normal life is the human nature to which we are divinely summoned, which is defined in terms of mutuality. This, at least, is the promise of biblical religion (p. 480)."

Fourth Opinion: I believe that all Christians, whether male or female, heterosexual or homosexual, celibate or non-celibate, married or single are called to intimacy with Jesus, and through him with the Mother-Father God, and that we are called to intimate or warm and loving relationships with others, and that these loving relationships will be sexual, whether in a genital or non-genital way.

All that being said, I wish to turn to more specific observations about celibacy, the religious life, and homosexuality. It is obvious from my experience as a major superior that these topics are important issues. However, I think they have always been important; it is just that we are dealing with these issues in a more open and less judgmental way than in the past.

In a recent discussion, a religious who had been director of a large house-of-formation program in the 1960s assured me that homosexuality in orientation and behavior has been a reality in our congregational houses of training for years. Now it seems there is or could be sufficient data to deal with this history and present reality more openly.

When discussing the issues of celibacy, religious life, and homosexuality, several distinctions are essential. First, the distinction between homosexual orientation or tendency and homosexual behavior is fundamental. As celibates, having an active genital lifestyle would be a contradiction to living the vowed life, whether this be in the context of a heterosexual or homosexual relationship.

If it is true, and it probably is, that more and more religious are experiencing serious difficulties in living a celibate lifestyle, then these individuals need to ask themselves challenging questions about their prayer life, community life, and their suitability to live a vowed life as a religious. Personally, I would experience great difficulty in living a celibate lifestyle without the support and concern of a caring community. I can well understand how difficult it must be for diocesan priests attempting to be celibate in an atmosphere of loneliness that often pervades our rectories. My personal opinion has been for a long time that diocesan priests should have the option to marry.

Secondly, I think we need to distinguish between a celibate engaging in a homosexually or heterosexually active lifestyle *and* a celibate discovering and dealing with his/her own sexuality. In other words, it is apparent that many religious have not even dealt with the important question of sexual orientation; therefore delayed adolescent kinds of experiences are quite possible while a person is discovering his/her sexual orientation and also trying to decide if he/she can continue to strive to live a celibate lifestyle.

Thirdly, it is important to distinguish between a homosexually active lifestyle and the fact that religious men and women will not always be able to live up to the demands of the ideal of celibacy. Those in positions of pastoral leadership would do well to be sensitive to this distinction.

These distinctions having been clarified, I would now like to offer some suggestions relating to ministry to homosexual men and women religious and candidates. A fundamental approach to people is to meet them where they are. If we do this, people will be more willing to share their joys, strengths, hurts, and weaknesses. It is only when people meet one another in this way that trust can be present and that genuine ministry can result.

According to Anthony Padovano:

> . . . ministry that seeks to satisfy only false, conventional needs is unreal and of service to no one. A person who engages in such a ministry becomes bored and is made artificial because nothing authentic is happening in his or her life. When ministry serves an institution to the detriment of the human person, it imprisons people, oppresses them, plays games with their needs (p. 9).

To meet the needs of dealing with one's own sexuality, I highly recommend the workshop offered by Donald

Ruedinger, M.D., medical director and president of Human Growth Center, Inc., Ann Arbor. Many of our brothers have made this workshop with sisters from various congregations during the summer in the renewal program offered by the Adrian Dominican Sisters at Weber Center in Michigan.

This workshop has been helpful in enabling our men to get in touch with their own sexuality and to risk meaningful and intimate, non-genital friendships with both women and men. It has facilitated a renewed appreciation of celibacy as a call to intimacy with the Lord and to non-genital, loving relationships with others.

Concerning admissions policies, I believe that no individual should automatically be excluded from entering religious life because of his/her homosexuality. What is important is how this person has integrated his/her sexuality and if he/she shows signs of a maturity that would indicate this person could make a realistic attempt at living a fulfilled and loving life as a celibate. Such issues as repressed anger, poor self-concept, and the inability to relate well with both men and women need to be discussed and reflected on before homosexual candidates are admitted to formation programs. I believe that as homosexuality is dealt with more honestly and openly, there will be more homosexual people who are well adjusted and who have come to terms with their homosexuality. I also believe that we already have homosexual religious who have been living loving lives as celibates for many years.

A real concern of mine is for the acceptance of homosexual religious in the context of our local religious communities. Several homosexual religious have shared with me their fear, anxiety, hurt, and guilt as they try to integrate themselves into communities where some members approach the topic with mockery and hostility. However, there are examples of individuals who have told their communities of their homosexual orientation and were personally accepted but challenged to integrate homosexuality into their lives.

It is unfortunate if our gay religious are forced to lead double lives, psychologically speaking, and to find their companionship in gay bars. Certainly, time and psychic energy invested in the gay subculture can threaten an individual's primary commitment to community and ministry.

Religious communities open to homosexual members, therefore, must ask fundamental questions of themselves if they are to live in growthful and celibate relationships. Are religious communities open, trusting, and comfortable enough with homosexual members and their friends? If not, then that community will have painful difficulties to deal with in assisting homosexual religious to be productive and happy members of the community.

Finally, I would like to underscore some issues suggested by Robert Nugent:

1. We need to spell out more clearly to ourselves and others those fundamental and underlying judgments we make about a homosexual orientation in and of itself. We will have to re-examine our personal and communal judgments about the homosexual orientation, hopefully with as much data as we can obtain from a variety of sources.

2. We will have to give much more study to the

distinction between orientation and behavior. I think especially in the Church we have concentrated almost entirely on behavior and have failed to develop our thinking on orientation and the impact it has on other areas of one's life. The question of public disclosure of one's homosexuality by clergy and religious is one that has to be addressed if we are to make any advance in ministry to those people in our communities and dioceses who are gay or lesbian in celibate commitments.

3. The third area we need to look at is the growing experience of support groups for priests and religious men and women, groups which are not organized to lobby, protest, recruit or demonstrate much less for sexual opportunities (an expressed fear in some quarters), but a group that can meet for discussion, prayer, reflection, support and even challenge in an atmosphere that is trusting and non-threatening.

4. The fourth area for development is the need for groups to be willing to tackle the issues and to validate the ministry regardless of the risks involved. . . . We are willing to identify with the poor and oppressed but not with homosexual people. We even fear the tensions that come when a community moves to educate the larger membership on the topic of homosexuality.

5. Fifth, we will have to explore the issue of ministry to gay and lesbian Catholics in general, and especially, ministry by those who feel called to such ministry.

6. We would do well to undertake a major study on homosexuality involving theologians from all perspectives, pastoral workers, social scientists, biblical scholars and gay and lesbian Christians.

In conclusion, I strongly believe religious men and women would do well to sponsor a major study on celibacy in the light of our new focus on celibacy as calling us to a way of loving, and not of avoiding love. Peter Cantwell, OFM, puts it well in the recent *Human Development* magazine:

> If celibacy by its nature demands a denial of intimacy, or closeness, as most of the definitions of yesteryear would imply, then it has no place in human growth, let alone as a gospel precept in a ministry, and theological research takes us beyond that stance, encouraging us to own our physical natures, to be at home without affective needs, and to express them appropriately. Celibacy can only be a positive value if it is a way of loving, not a way of avoiding love. It is through the genuine and integrated experience of intimacy that those qualities basic to ministry—gentleness, compassion, sensitivity, and warmth—come to fruition in the human being (p. 19).

References

Baum, G. Catholic homosexuals. *Commonweal,* 1974, 99 (19), 479–482.

Padovano, A. Our vulnerability needs ministry. *Forum: National Catholic Reporter,* October 23, 1981, 17 (45), 9–10, 18.

Cantwell, P. W. Ongoing growth through intimacy. *Human Development,* 1981, 2 (3), 14–20.

Chapter Eight

MORAL THEOLOGY AND HOMOSEXUALITY

Charles Curran

THIS chapter will consider the question of homosexuality from the perspective of moral theology in three different sections. The first part will discuss some aspects of moral theology with particular attention given to the relationship between moral theology and the Christian life. The second section will examine four different contemporary approaches in moral theology to the question of homosexuality. The final part will develop my own approach of moral theology to homosexuality.

I.

Moral theology as a discipline has been in the process of change and development in the last fifteen years. Many of these changes occurred in moral theology in terms of its general methodology and are very pertinent to the evaluation of the particular question of the morality of homosexuality and of homosexual acts. Catholic moral theology has traditionally employed the natural law approach, but within the discipline itself there has recently been much discussion about the precise meaning and adequacy of the natural law methodology. Natural law is a complex reality that involves at least two distinct questions from the perspective of moral methodology. The theological aspect of natural law concerns the sources in which Christian ethics finds ethical wisdom and knowledge. Natural law theory maintains the sources of moral theology are not only faith, revelation, and Jesus Christ but also, and even primarily, human reason and human nature. A very significant question then involves the exact relationship between faith and revelation, on the one hand, and reason and human nature, on the other hand. The philosophical aspect of the question of natural law refers to the precise meaning of human nature and human reason.[1]

A concomitant question in contemporary moral theology concerns the place of moral norms in the Christian life and the way in which norms are ultimately established. Some maintain that the existing norms (e.g., adultery is always wrong; remarriage after divorce is always wrong; torture is always wrong) have been arrived at in a deontological manner. The Christian conscience declares such actions are wrong and incompatible with Christian existence no matter what the consequences because the actions directly violate the order willed by God or go against fundamental goods and values in the Christian life. Others maintain that the existing norms have been established and should be justified (or questioned) on teleological grounds. The Christian community comes to the conclusion that certain actions are wrong because generally speaking no proportionate reason exists which would justify doing what is prohibited in these cases.[2] These methodological questions now being discussed in moral theology greatly influence the approach one takes to the question of homosexuality.

There are other significant methodological questions in moral theology that also have an important bearing on the approach to homosexuality. The proper way for the discipline to use the Sacred Scripture has received much attention in recent literature. All must recognize both the importance and the limitations of the scriptural witness for moral theology.[3] One very striking illustration of the problem involved in the use of Scripture in moral theology is found in the different liberation theologies. Latin American liberation theology makes strong appeal to the Scripture and finds there firm support for its position in the Exodus story, in the emphasis on the struggle against oppression and injustice, and in the privileged position of the poor.[4] Feminist liberation theology is confronted with a different reality. Here many parts of Scripture seem to support a basic inequality of the sexes. These differences point out the need for biblical theology and moral theology to employ a proper hermeneutic in understanding the data of the Scriptures and their relationship to contemporary reality.[5] Another significant problem concerns the use of the empirical sciences in moral theology. This question often comes to the fore in areas touching on economics, political science, sociology, and psychology. These two methdological questions assume significant importance in any ethical evaluation of homosexuality and of homosexual acts.[6]

Another very significant theoretical and practical question, especially in terms of life in the Christian community, concerns the relationship between church authority, moral theology and the life of the individual believer. All Christian churches claim an authority to preach the Word and describe the Christian way of life. Roman Catholic ecclesiology recognizes a special hierarchical teaching office in the church. Only in the last fifteen years have Catholic theologians and Catholic practice explicitly faced up to a discussion of the possibility of dissent from authoritative, authentic, non-infallible hierarchical teaching.[7] This chapter will prescind from this very important question.

These questions have been briefly mentioned at the beginning to indicate that a study of homosexuality must of its very nature also involve a discussion about the methodology to be employed in moral theology. The second part of this chapter will examine four different positions on homosexuality as well as the different methodologies employed in these positions. However, it will be impossible to examine at length all the methodological presuppositions of the four questions. Of necessity only the more salient and specific aspects of the methodologies will be discussed.

This first part will now explore in greater depth the relationship between moral theology and the living of the Christian life. Such a consideration should help to clarify what is the role and function of moral theology. The particular relationship under consideration is a variation of the broader question of the relationship between theory and practice.

In general, moral theology studies the Christian life and the way in which the Christian should live and act. From the very beginning, my understanding insists that moral theology must deal with more than just the moral evaluation of particular acts. Moral theology and Christian living involve much more than just actions. This discipline must also consider the attitudes, dispositions, and character of the Christian person. Also, goals, ideals, values, institutions, and structures form a very important part of moral theology. An older moral theology too often limited itself to a consideration of the morality of actions and usually to the minimal aspect of what constituted right and wrong.

Moral theology studies the Christian moral life, but every Christian is called upon to live the Christian life. Is every Christian a moral theologian? What relationship is there between studying the Christian life and living the Christian life?

Every single Christian is called upon to respond to the good news of God's love made present in Jesus Christ through the power of the Spirit. This response is often referred to in the Christian tradition in terms of the two-fold commandment of love—love of God and love of neighbor. All Christians are called through the gift of the Spirit to freely respond in conscience to this call. By our decisions and actions we make ourselves who we are. We shape our characters. In addition by our actions we try to bring about a greater peace and justice in the world in which we live. The Constitution on the Church of the Second Vatican Council maintains that all Christians are called to perfection and holiness.[8]

Perhaps the question can best be phrased in this manner: is the moral theologian a better living Christian than those who have never studied moral theology? A theologian must point out that such a question is somewhat crass and has Pelagian overtones, but the query focuses very well the issue to be discussed. The same question can be raised about any professional ethicist; i.e., one who studies ethics. Are ethicists better living people or better decision makers than those who have never systematically studied ethics?

From personal experience I can answer the question! Moral theologians are not necessarily the best living Christians. Ethicists are not necessarily the best living human beings and the best decision makers. An old spiritual axiom rightly maintains that it is much more important and significant to practice compassion than to be able to define compassion. There might be a tinge of anti-intellectualism in the axiom, but the basic reality is true. There are many very good living Christian people who have never studied moral theology. Many of us who have professionally studied moral theology would readily admit our failure to respond as we should to the gracious call of God in Jesus Christ.

What then is the relationship between moral theology and the living of the Christian life? Moral theology studies the Christian life in a systematic, thematic, and reflexive way. Moral theology involves second order discourse and seeks to understand the Christian moral life in a systematic way. But every Christian is called to live the fullness of the Christian life. Every Christian has the gift of the Spirit and is called to bring forth the fruits of the Spirit.

The Christian lives on the level of first order discourse and ordinarily does not stand back to reflect in a systematic, thematic and reflexive way on the Christian life. This does not mean that the Christian person should not be reflective about one's own life, but this reflection is not of a scientific nature involving the demands of consistency and coherency on the level of theory.

Perhaps an analogy will help to understand better the relationship between moral theology and the living of the Christian life. How do you respond to the following question? Are psychiatrists the most mature, emotionally well-balanced and developed people you know? Without denigrating a particular profession, most people would respond negatively to that question. Yet most people recognize that psychiatrists have a significant role to play at times in mental and emotional well-being. The psychiatrist studies systematically, thematically and reflexively the meaning of mental and emotional health and development. However, there are many people who have never read Freud or Jung or any theories of psychology and psychiatry who are emotionally mature and well-balanced human beings. What then is the role of psychiatry? Psychiatry studies on the level of second order discourse human emotional development and maturity. Especially when problems arise in one's psychic world, then the psychiatrist can try to help the individual to locate the problem and correct it. Psychiatry can contribute to a better understanding and better living of the human life, but every single human being possesses the basic human instinct to live an emotionally mature and well-balanced existence.

Moral theology has somewhat the same relationship to Christian moral life as psychiatry has to human emotional and psychic health. Moral theology operates on the level of theory trying to explain systematically and in a consistent and coherent way all the aspects of the moral life. People can lead good Christian lives without moral theology, but this discipline involves a critical approach of a scientific nature which helps in evaluating how Christians should live and act.

In keeping with the understanding of moral theology proposed here, the role of moral theology in the church will be less than the role often given to moral theology in the past. In the past the impression was often given that Christian practice was based on and followed from the theory developed in moral theology. The Catholic natural law theory was the basis on which it was decided that a particular practice or action was in conformity or not with the Christian understanding of human existence. There is some truth in this understanding. However, history would seem to indicate this was not always true. Many accepted practices in the church came about first, and only later was the natural law theory developed to explain the already existing moral practices. The Christian community itself in the light of all the help it has been given through the gift of the Spirit, including a hierarchical teaching function, came to the recognition that some actions were right and that other actions were wrong. The second order discourse of theory and systematization came later to explain in a systematic way why this particular action was right or wrong and how it fit in with an overall Christian understanding.

There is an analogy between the relationship of the individual Christian to moral theology and the relationship of the church as a whole to moral theology. The individual Christian by no means has to be a moral theologian but, moral theology offers help especially in time of crises and difficulties. The church itself has very often arrived at its own particular moral positions and teachings and then only later fully explained them and understood them in the light of a coherent and systematic theory. Moral theology is significant and important for critically understanding the Christian moral life. But this second order discourse with its insistence on a rigorous scientific development is not the only way in which the church comes to accept a particular practice or reject a particular practice or action.

The relationship between theory and practice in moral matters in the church today is reciprocal. Sometimes a new practice will come in and ultimately be accepted in the church community thereby calling for a change in the theory. The development which took place in the church's attitude to religious liberty well illustrates this reality. The lived experience and reality of religious liberty in the context of modern democratic societies came before the development of a theory to consistently and coherently explain this reality. The lived experience came first and only later was a theory developed to explain why the practice of religious liberty was consonant with Catholic self-understanding.[9]

However, not every new practice that comes along is necessarily good. Moral theology on the level of second order discourse, together with all the other moral insights available to the Christian community, can and should serve as a basis for rejecting some new possible developments and practices. The just war theory, for example, evolved in the Catholic tradition as a way of dealing with the morality of arms and warfare. The principle of discrimination in the just war theory forbids the direct killing of noncombatants. In the light of this theory the Second Vatican Council declared "any act of war aimed indiscriminately at the destruction of entire cities or extensive areas along with their populations is a crime against God and man himself. It merits unequivocal and unhesitating condemnation."[10] This theory rightly and strongly condemns using nuclear weapons against cities.

This reciprocal relationship between theory and practice is obviously operating in the contemporary discussions about sexuality in the life of the Roman Catholic Church and in moral theology. A glance at the literature of the past few years indicates how extensive the discussion has been. It is obvious that practice is changing within the Catholic Church on a number of questions dealing with human sexuality. The most obvious example is contraception. At the Synod of Bishops in Rome in 1980, Archbishop Quinn, the then President of the National Conference of Catholic Bishops, reported the figures from a study at Princeton University which concluded that 76.5 percent of married American Catholic women were using some form of birth regulation and that 94 percent of these women were using methods condemned by the church.[11] This changing practice has met with different theoretical reactions. Some have proposed a theory which accepts and justifies the practice, while other theologians condemn such practices on the basis of their theoretical understanding of moral theology and of human sexuality.[12] There can be no doubt that some of the recent developments and changes in the methodologies proposed in moral theology stem from a dissatisfaction with the past approach to questions of sexuality.

My understanding of moral theology recognizes that there is this reciprocal relationship between theory and practice so not only does theory have some influence on practice, but practice also has some influence on theory. The contemporary discussion on homosexuality takes place within this context. There is disagreement both about the morality of homosexuality and of homosexual acts and about the moral theory involved. A mutual relationship exists between one's approach to the theory of moral theology and the practical appreciation and understanding of homosexuality. The point is that one cannot discuss the question of homosexuality without also discussing the question of moral theology and its methodology. In the light of this understanding of moral theology and its relationship to life and practice, the second section of this chapter will examine different approaches to the meaning and morality of homosexuality and homosexual acts. One point needs to be repeated. This discussion is prescinding from the very significant question of the role of official hierarchical church teaching in relationship to both the moral life of the Christian and moral theology.

II.

This section will now consider and analyze four different approaches to the morality of homosexuality, paying attention both to the methodological approach taken by the various authors and to their substantive conclusions about homosexuality and homosexual acts. The four authors to be considered are: John Harvey; John McNeill; the authors of *Human Sexuality,* the Report of the Committee of the Catholic Theological Society of America; and Edward Malloy. The order of consideration is based on the chronological order of their writings.

John Harvey has been publishing in the area of homosexuality for over twenty-five years. No Catholic moral theologian has devoted more time or effort to this study. Perhaps the most synthetic discussion is his article in the *New Catholic Encyclopedia.*[13]

Harvey's methodological approach to the morality of homosexual acts is the natural law approach found in the manuals of moral theology. Homosexual acts are wrong because "such an act cannot fulfill the procreative purpose of the sexual faculty and is therefore an inordinate use of that faculty." This methodological approach begins with the recognition that every human person has a human nature, and one must live in accord with human nature. In human nature there are a number of built-in inclinations and faculties including the faculty of human sexuality. Human reason sees in the faculty the God given purpose and finality of procreation. Every sexual act must be open to the possibility of procreation. Human beings cannot directly go against the procreative purpose of human sexuality. Once procreation can be completely separated from the sexual act, then any kind of sexual act can be justified. The heavy emphasis is on the procreational aspect, and there is only a brief reference to going against the natural attraction of man for woman, which leads to the foundation of the basic stable unit of society, the family. The condemnation of homosexual acts in Scripture and in the traditional teaching of the church is in keeping with the reasons proposed.[14]

In addition to the question of the objective morality of homosexual acts, Harvey also considers the homosexual orientation itself and the subjective responsibility for homosexual actions. The homosexual orientation is not bad or evil, and the individual is not usually responsible for it. Sexual acts are always objectively wrong, but responsibility for these might be lessened because of circumstances that take away one's freedom. The pastoral solution is to develop self-control through asceticism and live a celibate existence.[15]

The critique of Harvey's theory will begin with consistency. In general his theory is consistent, coherent, and logically based on the nature and function of the sexual faculty. However, there is one point which might be raised against the consistency of the theory. Harvey admits that the homosexual condition itself is not wrong or evil. One could argue that the homosexual is truly acting in accord with one's nature and therefore is doing no wrong. Harvey would probably respond that human nature is not just the existing reality but the plan of right reason willed by God and found in the essential teleology of the sexual faculty itself. By benignly recognizing that the homosexual orientation is not evil in itself, Harvey might be giving some backing to the arguments of his opponents. In general, however, his theory is quite consistent.

My problem with his theory can be stated rather succinctly. The sexual faculty and acts should never be seen apart from the person and the person's relationship to other persons. I would argue that for the good of the person or for the good of the marital relationship one can interfere with the procreative aspect of the sexual act through the use of contraception. To see the meaning of human sexuality primarily in the nature and finality of the sexual faculty does not seem to give enough importance to the contributions of history and culture to the meaning of human sexuality. The theory tends to be ahistorical. I have often described this type of theory as being guilty of physicalism. The physical structure of the act becomes normative, and no one can ever interfere with the physical act. This problem comes to the fore especially in the theory's condemnation of artificial contraception. Harvey's theory serves to ground norms that are always obliging because they are based on the essential natural order willed by God. There is no room for possible exceptions or for the recognition that secondary precepts of the natural law oblige only as generally happens (*ut in pluribus*), and admit of exceptions in unique circumstances. Think of the famous case often mentioned in the literature of Christian ethics about Mrs. Bergmeier. In the story as first narrated by Joseph Fletcher, Mrs. Bergmeier seduced a prison guard and became pregnant so that as a result of her pregnant status she would be released from the horrors of the prison camp and sent home.[16]

A very important consideration concerns the relationship between sexuality and procreation. No one can deny (except for the cases of artificial insemination and *in vitro* fertilization) that procreation takes place through sexual relations. Traditional Roman Catholic moral theology has stressed procreation as an end or good of sexuality and has condemned artificial contraception as an unwarranted interference in the procreative nature of the sexual act. On the other hand, the Catholic Church has allowed sterile people to marry. In addition, there has been much development in terms of the understanding of the role of procreative intent in marriage and sexuality. At one time it was thought that only a procreative intent saved the sexual act in marriage from being wrong. Now it is accepted in Catholic teaching that husband and wife can intend that their sexual relations not be procreative and even purposely choose the time when the wife is not fertile. There is some relationship between sexuality and procreation, but that relationship is very difficult to define and very difficult to use as a criterion for an absolute moral condemnation.

John J. McNeill, a Jesuit priest, philosopher, and theologian wrote some articles on homosexuality in *The Homiletic and Pastoral Review* in 1970 and published *The Church and the Homosexual* in 1976. The book was finally published with ecclesiastical permission from his Jesuit superiors after a delay of two years. However, that permission itself was later rescinded.[17]

McNeill reacts to the overemphasis on nature, reason and law in the traditional approach to sexuality in moral theology. The human person is understood primarily in terms of radical freedom. The older approach has stressed the natural and biological rather than the personal which is truly what is unique about the human. Human sexuality participates in radical human freedom. Whatever participates in human freedom cannot receive its total explanation in terms of causal determinism. We are born male or female biologically speaking, but we become men or women through a free human process of education. What it means to be a man or woman in a given society or culture is a free human cultural creation. In the light of this emphasis on the person and on the freedom of the person, the basic moral norm for sexuality is love. A general consideration of the scriptural data leads to the same conclusion that sexual relations can be justified morally if they are a true expression of human love. Interpersonal love is the ideal human context for sexual expression. The practical norms governing human sexual expression are derived from the concept of the human person as an end in himself or herself and from the necessary conditions of possibility for genuine interpersonal love relationship. Among these conditions are such norms as mutuality, fidelity and unselfishness.[18]

McNeill logically must and does deal with two factors that have often been proposed as bases for the traditional position condemning homosexual acts—the procreative aspect of human sexuality and the male-female complementarity. The nature of the love relationship, not the procreative aspect, is the norm for sexual expression. His argument here is rather curious. The Catholic Church continues to condemn any voluntary separation of the coequal purposes of sexual behavior, procreation and mutual love. The genuine homosexual does not fall under this condemnation since the procreative aspect is not eliminated by a free voluntary choice of the individual. The homosexual couple should be compared with the sterile heterosexual couple who are not able to procreate.[19] I think a better case could be made primarily through disagreeing with the teaching that artificial contraception is always wrong. McNeill's own methodology logically cannot condemn artificial contraception. One can appreciate that he is trying to find arguments for a position within traditionally accepted Catholic teaching, but McNeill seems to be stretching too much and conceding too much with this particular argument.

Male-female complementarity cannot be proposed as the norm, nor as the God given reality, nor as the divine image in human existence. What makes one male or female is not biology but a free human cultural creation. In the course of history look at all the problems of the domination of the female by the male that have resulted from the apparently God given complementarity between male and female. The critical theologian should try to liberate humanity from these poor sexual stereotypes. The primary God-given ideal goal of human sexual development is that people should fashion cultural identities that make it possible for human beings to achieve the fullness of a true personal relationship of sexual love. Since it seems to be God's plan that ten percent of human beings do not conform to the accepted heterosexual pattern, these homosexual people should not be cut off from the goal of human sexual development in terms of a personal relationship of sexual love. To make the biological male-female complementarity the basis of the moral norm for sexuality would deny human freedom its important role.[20] In the light of this theory, McNeill maintains that for the genuine homosexual or the invert, which is the word he frequently uses, a sexual relationship characterized by mutuality, unselfishness, and fidelity is a good.

The Scriptures and tradition need to be properly interpreted in the light of historical, cultural, and psychological realities of their own times. The Scriptures condemn perverse homosexual activity engaged in by otherwise truly heterosexual individuals as an expression of contempt or self-centered lust and usually associated with some form of idol worship. Both the Scriptures and the historical tradition did not know the phenomenon of inversion, and therefore they cannot be judged as condemning the homosexual acts of genuine homosexual inverts in the context of a loving relationship.[21] *The Church and the Homosexual* also cites data from the human sciences to indicate that many homosexuals have avoided the traps of promiscuity and depersonalized sex by entering into mature homosexual relationships with one partner and with the intention of fidelity and mutual support.[22]

In terms of critique, there is an overall consistency to McNeill's approach with its emphasis on freedom and love and the denial of the procreative aspect and the male-female complementarity. However, I have some disagreements with McNeill's concept of the person as radical freedom and think there is some problem of consistency in his own approach. McNeill insists on understanding the person in terms of radical freedom. On the other hand he is inclined to agree with the position that the homosexual condition "is the result of an unconscious psychological process which lies radically outside the conscious, and therefore, free self-determination of the individual."[23] If there are certain aspects of our makeup and sexuality that we can't change, then our freedom is not as radical as this author claims. In addition, the Jesuit theologian justifies homosexual acts only for the genuine homosexual or invert. However, if the human person is to be defined in terms of radical freedom alone, it would seem that one must consistently also accept the fact that such actions could also be justified for the person who is not a genuine homosexual. It seems that the sexual orientation of the person as well as freedom enter into McNeill's own position. I agree that there are many things about ourselves that we cannot change, but as a result one has to conclude that our freedom is more limited and situated.

My basic philosophical disagreement with McNeill centers on this question of anthropology. In my judgment, human freedom is more situated and limited. Consider human experience. Human beings are quite limited by our heredity and our environment. All people experience tiredness and fatigue. We cannot for a long time avoid the basic human need for rest and recreation. We are limited by our bodies to being in only one place at one time. Some existential thinkers see human choice as a sacrifice. When we choose to do one thing, we recognize our limitations and inabilities to do many other possible choices at the same time. Yes, we have freedom in the sense of determining our own fate through our actions, but we are also limited by our multiple relationships with others, the world, and even with ourselves. In terms of our relationship with the world, the whole ecological debate has made us aware that our freedom is very limited. Too often in the past, in the name of freedom and self-determination, human beings have abused the finite resources of our planet earth and the complex ecosystems that are present and necessary for our world.

Contemporary theology has also been discussing the

understanding of the human person. Johannes Metz disagrees with the transcendental Thomism of his mentor Karl Rahner with its primary emphasis on the freedom of the self-transcending subject. Such a position according to Metz fails to give enough importance to the political and social aspects of reality.[24] I, too, agree that human anthropology cannot be reduced to radical freedom because human freedom is more situated and limited and more importance must be given to the social, political, and cosmic dimensions of human existence.

McNeill's anthropology logically sees sexuality in terms of radical human freedom. My anthropology gives more importance to the structures of human sexuality. Human sexuality is an embodied sexuality, and embodiment remains an important part of human sexuality as such. Too often radical freedom can imply a dualism between spirit and body in the human being. Body is an important aspect of all human anthropology. The embodiment of human sexuality in terms of male-female differences and complementarity is an important aspect of the meaning of human sexuality. Unfortunately, this complementarity too often in the past has been used by males to dominate females. But complementarity of itself does not necessarily involve the use of stereotypical sex roles which have been so prejudicial to women. Male-female complementarity is a part of human sexuality, for our sexuality is an embodied sexuality and our anthropology is an embodied anthropology. As a consequence, I do not accept McNeill's contention that male-female complementarity does not enter into the meaning of human sexuality and the norms governing human sexuality.

A third approach to homosexuality is that published

by the Committee on the Study of Human Sexuality of the Catholic Theological Society of America, published under the title *Human Sexuality: New Directions in American Catholic Thought.*[25] The authors, Anthony Kosnik, William Carroll, Agnes Cunningham, Ronald Modras, and James Schulte refer to homosexuality in the context of their broader discussion. Their approach logically begins with a definition of human sexuality and its meaning. These authors insist on an embodied view of human existence. Subjectivity is embodied in either a male or female. Kosnik *et al.* are of the opinion that the two sexes experience themselves in subtly different ways by reason of their differences in bodily structure. The genital impulse is predisposed in favor of heterosexual union. It is in the genital union that the intertwining of subjectivities of human existence has the potential for fullest realization.[26]

The next step involves the approach to be taken in determining moral norms governing sexuality. There are three different levels of moral evaluation. The first level is that of the universal principle which governs all of human sexuality and is described as the need for sexuality to serve creative growth toward integration. The second level of moral evaluation describes the particular moral values associated with sexuality—self-liberation, other enrichment, honesty, fidelity, service to life, social responsibility, and joy. The third level of moral evaluation concerns the concrete norms, rules, precepts or guidelines which govern human sexuality in light of protecting the values of human sexuality mentioned above. These norms indicate what Christian experience has proven to occur generally (*ut in pluribus*). To the extent these norms refer to concrete physical actions (e.g., masturbation) without specifying particular circumstances or intentions, they cannot be regarded as universal or absolute moral norms.[27] In reviewing the literature on homosexuality, the book summarizes four different approaches to the question: (1) Homosexual acts are intrinsically evil. (2) Homosexual acts are essentially imperfect. (3) Homosexual acts are to be evaluated in terms of their relational significance. (4) Homosexual acts are essentially good and natural. The authors exclude both the first and the fourth solutions. They express some problems with both the second and the third approaches, but these approaches are more compatible with the understanding of sexuality developed in their report.[28]

My primary negative criticism of this approach is the lack of consistency. In developing the meaning of human sexuality, the report emphasizes the male and female aspects of human sexuality and the complementarity involved. However, the seven values of human sexuality, which constitute the second level of the moral evaluation, do not incorporate the male and female aspects of sexuality. If maleness and femaleness are so significant for the meaning of human sexuality, it should appear in the values that are to be found and protected in sexuality. The book opts for either the second or third of the four positions found in the contemporary literature. The second position makes heterosexual relationships the ideal, but the third position bases everything on the quality of the relationship. This third position logically follows on the basis of the seven values of human sexuality posed in the moral evaluation. But on the basis of the insistence on the male-female complementarity in the definition of human sexuality, the authors would logically have to reject the third position.

The crux of the inconsistency is that the meaning of sexuality accepts a male-female complementarity, but the values of sexuality do not seem to incorporate this reality. For this reason one can rightly criticize the values proposed for being overly general and not specifically referring to human sexuality as such in all its specifics. One could argue that very many different human realities should embody these same seven basic values.

Edward A. Malloy has developed a fourth approach to homosexuality in his recent book, *Homosexuality and the Christian Way of Life.*[29] In his own words Malloy characterizes his book as a response to the revisionists. The revisionists are those who have proposed that homosexual acts in the context of a faithful, stable, mutual relationship can be morally justified and acceptable. Malloy believes that the revisionists have not made their case and sets out to prove that claim in his book.[30]

Malloy compares the homosexual way of life with the Christian way of life. He concludes the section of the book on the homosexual way of life in this way:

> The central claim of this first section of the book can be phrased in the following manner. The homosexual way of life is a pattern of social organization that takes certain characteristic forms which find a common focus in the ultimate commitment to unrestricted personal sexual freedom. Whatever other values individual homosexuals may hold and pursue, this liberation conviction is at the heart of their common identity with other homosexuals. To accept homosexuality as a way

> of life is to call into question any attempt to enforce sexual standards of a more restrictive sort, whether based on political, social or religious grounds.[31]

The Christian way of life inculcates three virtues in the realm of sexuality. Chastity is the disciplined determination of appropriate sexual behavior according to the degree of the relationship of the partners. Love is the ultimate sharing of mutual concern according to the natural stages of attraction, passion, friendship, and sacrificial service. Faithfulness to promise involves the patient endurance and the voluntary exchange of the reciprocal commitment according to the community-based meaning of exclusivity and permanence. In the light of these values the church has seen monogamous marriage as the context that best promotes full realization of sexual expression. The homosexual way of life as described earlier is irreconcilable with the Christian way of life, for it is opposed to the three basic values of chastity, love, and faithfulness. Some individual homosexuals may achieve these virtues, but it is in spite of the homosexual way of life. The homosexual way of life is centered on the pursuit of unrestricted sexual pleasure.[32]

Malloy devotes a chapter to explaining and refuting the position of the ethical revisionists whom he divides into the moderate revisionists, who accept homosexual acts within a stable, exclusive relationship, and radical revisionists. The chapter maintains that the revisionists have not won the day, and their arguments are not convincing.[33] In the closing section on pastoral responses to the homosexual, Malloy admits that homosexual couples consciously committed to a permanent and exclusive relationship offer the best hope for the preservation of

Christian values by active homosexuals. For those incapable of a celibate existence such a private arrangement is preferable to the other alternatives. However, the celibate option for Christian homosexuals should continue to be presented as the most consistent response to the Christian ethical view.[34]

My primary negative criticism of Malloy is his failure to really join the issue. No Catholic moral theologian defends the homosexual way of life as he has described it and defined it. In condemning the homosexual way of life he is really condemning a straw person and not entering into true dialogue with other theologians on this issue. There is also a problem with the way in which he has divided revisionists into moderate and radical revisionists. According to him, moderate revisionists are those who maintain the need for a stable and faithful relationship. However, he never properly distinguishes the radical revisionists from the moderate revisionists. Malloy puts both McNeill and Kosnik *et al.* under the category of radical revisionists, but both of them also insist very much on the importance of a mutual, faithful relationship. Also, this reader was somewhat surprised to read in the final pastoral section at the end of the book some limited acceptance of homosexual couples committed to a permanent and exclusive relationship. Nothing in the book really prepares the reader for this. Such a position is crying out for further elucidation especially in the light of everything else that Malloy has said. How does this position differ from the moderate revisionist position? What is the basis for such a pastoral practice? What exactly does he mean by the possibility of limited acceptance of such a relationship?

In my judgment a very significant difference between

Malloy and the revisionists is the assumption about the possibility of a homosexual couple living in a faithful and exclusive relationship. Malloy implies this is possible only for a very few. The revisionists maintain there is a greater possibility for such relationships especially if they can be openly accepted and supported both in society and in the church.

III.

Since I have developed my own approach to homosexuality in previous publications, there is no need to repeat what has been said before.[35] This section will briefly set forth my own position and then try to respond to some of the objections that have been, or can be, brought up against it.

My position affirms that for an irreversible, constitutional, or genuine homosexual, homosexual acts in the context of a loving relationship striving for permanency are objectively morally good. On the other hand, the ideal meaning of human sexual relationships is in terms of male and female. My assumption is that the genuine homosexual orientation is irreversible. Those who can must strive for heterosexual orientation, but this is not possible for the genuine or irreversible homosexual.

This position on homosexuality fits into a broader theory—a theory or theology of compromise. According to this theory, because of the presence of the sin of the world, Christians are justified in doing certain acts which would not be justified without the presence of such sin of the world. In the past many Catholic theologians justified private property on the basis of the presence of sin in the world and maintained that, if there were no such sin, there would be no private property.

Note well that the sin of the world does not refer to personal guilt, fault, or sin. The objective condition is existing independently of one's own responsibility or guilt. But this objective situation is not a good. It is an evil, but not a moral evil. Christians are called, in general, to struggle against such evil, but it is not always possible to overcome it. Consider again the justification and acceptance of private property. Such is the case of the genuine and irreversible homosexual.

Perhaps this position can be clarified in the process of responding to objections. As a mediating position, this approach can be questioned both by those who hold to the traditionally accepted approach and by those who hold for a more radical position.

How can one abandon the traditional approach which has been existing in the church for so long? Our knowledge of psychology has only developed in comparatively recent times. We know much more today than we ever did before about the human psyche and the human person. The genuine or constitutional homosexual is a reality that was explicitly unknown in the past. Within the Catholic theological tradition, John Harvey made a great innovation by emphasizing the distinction between the homosexual orientation and the homosexual act. The literature of moral theology was not even explicitly aware of this distinction until very recently. Obviously my own approach would go further than that of Harvey, but it is based ultimately on an understanding coming to us from the human sciences which was unavailable to those who lived earlier. Also the official church teaching has changed significantly in the importance it now gives to the relationality aspect of sexuality.

If a permanent homosexual orientation can justify

homosexual acts of the person, what about other orientations? Does the permanent attraction or orientation to animals justify beastiality? What about child molesting? Recall that not all the acts of the constitutional homosexual are justified. These acts must be seen within the context of a loving, faithful relationship striving for permanency. It is precisely this relationship which is missing in the other cases.

But does God not give people the strength and the grace to keep his law? If the orientation is somehow connected with the sin of the world, should not the Christian be able to overcome it with God's help? Perhaps an analogy will help. The possibility of the moral justification of going to war, which has long been held in the Catholic theological tradition, obviously is related to the sin of the world. All are called to work for peace, but resort to arms as a last resort has always been an acceptable option for Christians in this world. The fullness of the kingdom is not yet here. Those who think the moderate revisionist position goes too far must maintain that all constitutional homosexuals are called by God to celibacy. I believe that celibacy is a charism in the church given to certain individuals, but it is not automatically given to all people with a permanent homosexual orientation.

The more radical position also raises objections. Why are heterosexuality and heterosexual acts the ideal? Why is it necessary even to postulate an ideal? I interpret the Scriptures and the tradition as pointing to the ideal meaning of human sexuality as involving the complementarity of male and female. My understanding of human sexuality as embodied also comes to the conclusion that male-female complementarity is the ideal meaning of human sexuality. Also there are social and pastoral reasons supporting heterosexuality as the ideal. In the process of psycho-sexual development many people go through different phases, including at times a homosexual phase. Heterosexuality as the ideal gives a direction and guide in this process of development.

Does this position still treat homosexuals as second class people? All persons are to be respected as persons. Homosexuality should not be identified with personality. Homosexuality is not the ideal, but this does not mean that the person is of less dignity. One might make a comparison with the ideal of human existence as meaning a human being with all one's limbs and faculties. To be blind or deaf or missing an arm is not the ideal. It is a real lack, but this in no way affects the equal dignity of the person. So too in the case of homosexuality; the person as such is still deserving of just as much respect as any other person.

Why employ the term and the understanding of sin of the world? There is no doubt that reference to the sin of the world can cause some problems. But the sin of the world refers to the sinful structures and realities present in our world and in no way to personal guilt, blame, or responsibility. The phrase "sin of the world" is used to emphasize that heterosexuality is the ideal. I want to distinguish carefully between finitude and sin. Some moral theologians today are not that insistent on making clear this distinction between finitude and sin.[36] In my judgment there are both important theoretical and practical reasons for so doing. There is a difference between finitude and sin. The Roman Catholic theological tradition has recognized that there is a form of human limitation which comes from finitude, but there is another form of limitation which comes from sin. The distinction also has practical ramifications. Finitude is part of our make-up and will always characterize human existence in this world. The reality of finitude is not something less than the ideal. The sin of the world bespeaks a true lack—something which falls short of the human ideal. My use of the term sin of the world is connected with the understanding of heterosexuality as the ideal. However, for the constitutional homosexual, homosexual acts in the context of a loving relationship striving for permanency are objectively morally good.

This chapter has attempted to discuss homosexuality from the perspective of moral theology. The first section considered some aspects of moral theology itself, especially the relationship between theory and moral life. The second part examined and critiqued four different approaches to the question while the final section has proposed and explained my own mediating position.

Notes

1. For my position, see my *Themes in Fundamental Moral Theology* (Notre Dame, Ind.: University of Notre Dame Press, 1977), pp. 27–80. For a different approach, see William E. May, "Natural Law and Objective Morality: A Thomistic Perspective," in *Principles of Catholic Moral Life,* ed. William E. May (Chicago: Franciscan Herald Press, 1980), pp. 151–190. The best source for a review and critique of developments in moral theology in the last fifteen years is Richard A. McCormick, *Notes on Moral Theology 1965 through 1980* (Washington, D.C.: University Press of America, 1981).

2. For different approaches to this question, see *Readings in Moral Theology No. 1: Moral Norms and Catholic Tradition,* ed. Charles E. Curran and Richard A. McCormick (New York: Paulist Press, 1979).

3. See Bruce C. Birch and Larry L. Rasmussen, *Bible and Ethics in the Christian Life* (Minneapolis, Minn.: Augsburg Publishing House, 1976).

4. Anthony J. Tambasco, *Juan Luis Segundo and First-World Ethics: The Bible for Ethics* (Washington, D.C.: University Press of America, 1981).

5. Elizabeth Schüssler-Fiorenza, "New Testament Ethics and Early Christian Ethos: A Feminist Theological Perspective," to be published in *The Annals of the Society of Christian Ethics 1982.*

6. I have discussed both of these methodological questions in the context of the question of homosexuality in my *Catholic Moral Theology in Dialogue,* paperback ed. (Notre Dame, Ind.: University of Notre Dame Press, 1976), pp. 186–197.

7. *Readings in Moral Theology No. 3: The Magisterium and Morality,* ed. Charles E. Curran and Richard A. McCormick (New York: Paulist Press, 1982).

8. Constitution on the Church, Chapter V, par. 39–42.

9. Richard J. Regan, *Conflict and Consensus: Religious Freedom and the Second Vatican Council* (New York: Macmillan Co., 1967). The Declaration on Religious Freedom itself begins with the recognition of the demand and the desire of contemporary people for religious liberty, and it declares these desires to be greatly in accord with truth and justice.

10. Pastoral Constitution on the Church in the Modern World, par. 80.

11. Archbishop John R. Quinn, "New Context for Contraception Teaching," *Origins: N.C. Documentary Service* 10 (October 9, 1980), 263–267.

12. Joseph A. Selling, "The Reaction to *Humanae Vitae:* A Study in Special and Fundamental Theology" (S.T.D. diss., Catholic University of Louvain, 1977).

13. John F. Harvey, "Homosexuality," *New Catholic Encyclopedia* (New York: McGraw-Hill, 1967), VII, pp. 116–119. For Harvey's criticism of some contemporary approaches, see John F. Harvey, "Contemporary Theological Views," in John R. Cavanagh, *Counseling the Homosexual* (Huntington, Ind.: Our Sunday Visitor Press, 1977), pp. 222–238.

14. Harvey, *New Catholic Encyclopedia,* VII, pp. 117–118.

15. *Ibid.*

16. Joseph Fletcher, *Situation Ethics: The New Morality* (Philadelphia: Westminster Press, 1966), pp. 164–165.

17. John J. McNeill, "The Christian Male Homosexual," *The Homiletic and Pastoral Review* 70 (1970), 667–677; 747–758; 828–

836; *The Church and the Homosexual* (New York: Pocket Books, 1978).

18. *The Church and the Homosexual,* pp. 111–117; 207–208.

19. *Ibid.,* pp. 110–111.

20. *Ibid.,* pp. 114–116.

21. *Ibid.,* pp. 76–77.

22. *Ibid.,* pp. 77; 118–135. It should be pointed out in passing that McNeill develops his approach in dialogue with and in distinction from my own theory (*Ibid.,* pp. 41–47). However, McNeill has misinterpreted my position. For confirmation of this, see Lisa Sowle Cahill, "Homosexuality," in *Homosexuality and Ethics,* ed. Edward Batchelor, Jr. (New York: Pilgrim Press, 1980), pp. 225–227.

23. *Ibid.,* p. 190.

24. Johannes B. Metz, *Theology of the World* (New York: Herder and Herder, 1969), pp. 107–125, Metz, "Forward," in Karl Rahner, *Spirit in the World* (New York: Herder and Herder, 1968), pp. XIII–XVIIII.

25. Anthony Kosnik, William Carroll, Agnes Cunningham, Ronald Modras, James Schulte, *Human Sexuality: New Directions in American Catholic Thought* (New York: Paulist Press, 1977).

26. *Ibid.,* pp. 82–85.

27. *Ibid.,* pp. 96–97.

28. *Ibid.,* pp. 200–209.

29. Edward A. Malloy, *Homosexuality and the Christian Way of Life* (Washington, D.C.: University Press of America, 1981).

30. *Ibid.,* pp. viii–ix.

31. *Ibid.,* p. 181.

32. *Ibid.,* pp. 322–328.

33. *Ibid.,* pp. 243–286.

34. *Ibid.,* pp. 359–360.

35. *Catholic Moral Theology in Dialogue,* pp. 184–219; *Transition and Tradition in Moral Theology* (Notre Dame, Ind.: University of Notre Dame Press, 1979), pp. 59–80.

36. Joseph Fuchs, "The Sin of the World and Normative Morality," *Gregorianum* 61 (1980), 60.

Epilogue

SHIFTING ATTITUDES TOWARD HOMOSEXUALITY

Kenneth McGuire, C.S.P.

THE question of how Roman Catholic ministers deal with homosexuality has become more public in the last five or six years. In late October, 1982 the *Los Angeles Times* reported that former Vice-President Walter Mondale spoke before a gay political group in New York City. That a national political figure would address a gay group represented a marked break from tradition. Increasingly, political candidates have become conscious of the gay vote. The same week *Time* and *Newsweek* published articles about the report from the San Francisco Archdiocesan Task Force on Homosexuality. Homosexuality is no longer a private concern.

Over the past three decades the trend in publications reveals startling changes. Until 1955 neither the *Reader's Guide to Periodical Literature* nor the *Catholic Periodical and Literature Index* listed homosexuality as a category. Instead, such articles were indexed under "Sex Perversion." When homosexuality was first recorded as a distinct category, there were only a few articles in even fewer magazines which dealt with the topic. The trend remained unchanged until a slight increase occurred in 1963 and 1964. During those two years about 30 articles on the subject appeared. This significant increase was followed by a continued gradual increase until 1977 when the number of magazines and articles dramatically doubled from the previous year. During the 1970s, 86 magazines collectively carried 430 articles on homosexuality. The taboo topic was stepping out of the closet.

By 1980 the religious and secular press had exposed many Catholics to problems, questions, and debates about homosexuality. Campus ministers, administrators, pastors, counselors, confessors—in fact, almost every kind of minister in the Roman Catholic Church —encountered the issue. Homosexuality was being approached as a minority, moral, and justice issue.

The Roman Catholic position on the morality of homosexuality was developed by a distinction between homosexual orientation and homosexual acts. Individual bishops and bishops' conferences issued reports and pastoral letters; diocesan gay ministry task forces were formed. Because theological opinions differed, support or opposition for a variety of options could be cited. Such was the climate in which the First National Symposium on Homosexuality and the Catholic Church was convened.

Yet, even as attitudes on the whole were shifting toward a more open and free exchange, one incident at the symposium reveals the fear and anxiety which many well-intentioned Christians must face. In a conversation between two symposium participants, one confided to the other: "When I drove into the parking garage, I asked the attendant where to park for the conference. He asked, 'Which conference?' I had a difficult time saying 'The homosexual symposium.'"

The other participant was consoling: "Well, that's all right. I walked up to the front desk and asked where the major conference room was located. The clerk asked, 'Which one?' and all I could do was to point to the brochure and say, 'This one.'"

In addition to providing an excellent series of papers which are contained in this book, the symposium offered an opportunity to sample a group of Roman Catholic leaders concerned about this sensitive issue. What were their views or opinions? Symposium participants were asked to fill out a brief survey. Of approximately 180 symposium participants, 102 returned the questionnaire. Although conference registration forms indicated that three-fourths of the participants were national or diocesan church leaders, some of the conference attendees were novices, seminarians, students or Dignity members.

To obtain a picture of attitudes among some major church superiors, I considered a subset of the returned questionnaires. Of the 66 major congregational administrators or formation personnel in attendance at the symposium, 51 responded to the questionnaire. This 77 percent response rate is extremely high for sociological surveys. Therefore, the survey results are fairly reliable for assessing the views of those congregational leaders in attendance.

Of these leaders of religious communities 82 percent indicated that they had a sufficient understanding of the church's teaching position regarding homosexuality; however, approximately the same percentage believed that this position was inadequate. Only 2 religious administrators responded that the church's moral position was adequate. Similarly, about 65 percent of the congregational leaders stated that they sufficiently understood the Catholic Church's pastoral position on homosexuality, but an even greater percentage was unwilling to defend the adequacy of the church's pastoral approach.

Obviously, most of the religious congregational leadership attending the symposium were searching for a more sensitive and compassionate development of official church views on moral and pastoral guidelines regarding homosexuality. What factors had prompted these church superiors to look for more compassionate approaches? Many indicated that reading such books as John Boswell's *Christianity, Social Tolerance and Homosexuality* or *Human Sexuality* by the Committee on Sexuality from the Catholic Theological Society of America had been instrumental in forming their attitudes toward homosexuality. Others mentioned Wood's *Another Kind of Love,* Tripp's *The Homosexual Matrix* and publications from New Ways Ministry. The book cited most often as significant in forming their views was John McNeill's *The Church and the Homosexual.* Since each of these books and several others named have been published since the mid 1970s, it seems that there has been a substantial shift in the attitudes of major church leaders in fairly short and recent time.

Not only reading but also personal experience was named as playing a prominent role in attitude formation. Many major administrators and formation personnel spoke of personal friendships with students or ex-religious who had struggled with their sexuality and who were now striving to live in committed homosexual relationships. They acknowledged that meeting and getting to know lesbian and gay people whom they respected and admired and who have integrated their sexual identity within their Christian lives had enabled these church leaders to question the myths and stereotypes which they had been socialized to accept. Some remarked on their experiences in counseling, spiritual direction or therapy with gay teenagers or adults.

There may be an unconscious fear on the part of some religious leaders, whether the fear is personal or whether it involves the public image of the community, to admit that homosexual people are in their own midst. But many provincials, councilors or formation personnel attending the symposium admitted that they had counseled gay religious or worked with nuns struggling with their sexual identity. These conversations and personal dealings with lesbian or gay community members contributed insights into the issue and helped to reshape their own attitudes. Finally, a few congregational leaders disclosed their own sexual attractions toward members of the same gender; their eventual acceptance of their own homosexual natures enabled them to reformulate their attitudes toward the Catholic Church's moral and pastoral positions on homosexuality.

Needless to say, such liberal and open attitudes do not necessarily characterize all major leaders of women's and men's religious institutes. The more progressive religious administrators were more likely to attend. However, what can be said with certainty is that more than 50 different religious congregations which were represented at the First National Symposium on Homosexuality and the Catholic Church are willing to rethink the church's traditional posture toward homosexuality.

For many church leaders the church's traditional stance does not offer sufficient guidance at this point in history in which attitudinal shifts are occurring. Congregational leaders are becoming increasingly more willing to take a "bottom-up" instead of "top-down" approach to homosexuality by listening to the lived experience of lesbian and gay people. As Carter Heyward expressed so well: "We have a long way to go. It is a frightening time of spiritual and sexual transformation in which our consciousness of who we are—individually and collectively—is expanding. We must be careful. We must be tender. We must be open to new discovery.[1] Church leaders are becoming open and committed to new discovery.

Notes

1. Carter Heyward, "Theological Explorations of Homosexuality," *The Witness,* 62:15, June, 1979.

About the Authors

ANN BORDEN served as secretary and president of Dignity/Philadelphia and co-chaired the 1981 Biennial International Convention of Dignity, Inc., an organization of lesbian and gay Catholics.

CHARLES CURRAN is a priest of the Rochester diocese, a Professor of Moral Theology at the Catholic University of America, and author of more than a dozen books on morality and ethics.

JEANNINE GRAMICK, a School Sister of Notre Dame, is a co-founder and co-director of New Ways Ministry. She recently completed a sociological study of lesbian women.

CORNELIUS HUBBUCH is the past Provincial of the American Central Province of the Xaverian Brothers and Secretary-Treasurer of the Conference of Major Superiors of Men.

THERESA KANE is President of the Sisters of Mercy of the Union, past President of the Leadership Conference of Women Religious and attained world notice by her address to Pope John Paul II during his

1979 visit to the United States in asking that the church open all forms of ministry to women.

KENNETH McGUIRE is a Paulist priest, an anthropologist, associate director of the Paulist Institute for Religious Research, and pastor of St. Mark's university parish at the University of California at Santa Barbara. He has written on topics of spirituality and sociological aspects of church life.

BRIAN McNAUGHT is an award winning writer, a lecturer and a certified sex counselor. In 1976 he was a delegate at the U.S. Bishops' Call to Action conference in Detroit to represent the concerns of gay Catholics.

ROBERT NUGENT, a Salvatorian priest, is a co-founder and co-director of New Ways Ministry. He has written and lectured extensively on pastoral aspects of gay ministry.

BARBARA ZANOTTI, a past Core Commissioner of the Women's Ordination Conference, is a feminist theologian specializing in the field of ethics and international relations. She has lectured and published on issues of feminism and peace.